D0295494

100 Years of Wildlife

100 Years of Wildlife

MICHAEL BRIGHT

This book is published to accompany the television series entitled *100 Years of Wildlife*, first broadcast in 2007

10 9 8 7 6 5 4 3 2 1

Published in 2007 by BBC Books, an imprint of Ebury Publishing
A Random House Group Company

The Random House Group Limited Reg. No. 954009

Addresses for companies within the Random House Group can be found at www.randomhouse.co.uk

A CIP catalogue record for this book is available from the British Library.

ISBN 978 1 846 07321 2

The Random House Group Limited makes every effort to ensure that the papers used in our books are made from trees that have been legally sourced from well-managed and credibly certified forests. Our paper procurement policy can be found on www.randomhouse.co.uk

To buy books by your favourite authors and register for offers visit www.rbooks.co.uk

Commissioning editor: Shirley Patton
Project editor: Eleanor Maxfield
Copy-editor: Caroline Taggart
Designer: Lisa Pettibone
Picture researcher: Lucie Muir/Wildscreen
Production controller: David Brimble

Colour origination, printing and binding by Butler and Tanner, Frome, England

Picture Credits

All pictures copyright BBC except for:
p.11 & 13 Cherry Kearton; p.14 Science and Society Library; p.15(l) Royal Photographic Society; p.15(r) Mary Evans/Douglas McCarthy; p.17–19 Martin and Osa Johnson Safari Museum; p.23 NMPFT/ Science and Society Picture Library; p.25 David Attenborough; p.32 Lady Philippa Scott; p.34–5 Eric Ashby; p.36–7 David Attenborough; p. 40 Tony Soper; p.41 David Attenborough; p.44–5 Armand Denis; p.51(t&r) Angela Scott/naturepl.com; p.53 BBC Natural History Unit; p.57 John Sparks/naturepl.com; p.59 Nigel Marven/naturepl.com; p.61 N.Shigeta/The Yomiuri Shimbun; p.62 BBC Wildlife Magazine; p.66/7 Sue Flood/naturepl.com; p.68 Huw Cordey/naturepl.com; p.71 Nigel Marven/naturepl.com; p.76–7 Ben Osborne/naturepl.com; p.81 BBC Natural History Unit; p.83 Martin Saunders; p.85 Ben Osborne/naturepl.com; p.89 Sue Flood/naturepl.com; p.90 Doug Allan/naturepl.com; p.96 Mike Salisbury/BBC Natural History Unit; p.96–7 Martha Holmes/naturepl.com; p.100/101 Huw Cordey/ naturepl.com; p.103(t) Neil Nightingale/naturepl.com; 103(b) Konstantin Mikhailov/naturepl.com; p.105 Bruce Davidson/naturepl.com; p.106 BBC NHU; p.109 Doug Allan/naturepl.com; p.110 Ben Osborne/ naturepl.com; p.112(t&b) Mark Brownlow/naturepl.com; p.115 Alan Root; p.116 Minden Pictures/Franz Lanting; p.119 John Sparks; p.121 osfimages.com; p.126 Richard Kirby; p.128 Peter Bassett/naturepl.com; p.129(t) John Downer Productions/naturepl.com; p.129(b) John Downer/naturepl.com; p.130 John Downer Productions/naturepl.com; p.131 right John Downer/naturepl.com; p.132 Mark Payne-Gill/ naturepl.com; p.134 Martin Dohrn/naturepl.com; p.136 John Downer/naturepl.com; p.137 Robert Fulton/naturepl.com; p.139 Sue Flood/naturepl.com; p.142 Hans Hass Archive HIST/BBC Natural History Unit; p.147 Jeff Rotman/naturepl.com; p.152 Tom Walmsley/naturepl.com; p.153 osfimages.com; p.154 Mark Brownlow/naturepl.com; p.156 Sue Flood/naturepl.com; p.157 Georgette Douwma/ naturepl.com; p.159 David Shale/naturepl.com; p.160 Doug Allan/naturepl.com; p.161 Ben Osborne/ naturepl.com; p.163 osfimages.com; p.164 Neil P. Lucas/naturepl.com; p.165 John Sparks/naturepl.com; p.166 BBC Natural History Unit; p.170–1 Ben Osborne/naturepl.com; p.174 Karen Bass/BBC Natural History Unit; p.177 Keith Scholey/naturepl.com; p.182 Phil Agland; p.183 Neil Nightingale/ naturepl.com; p.184 Ben Osborne/naturepl.com; p.185 Neil Lucas/naturepl.com

Contents

Introduction

WILDLIFE FILMMAKING is a funny business. For the uninitiated, it may seem a wonderful way to make a living, but the reality is something altogether different. The late Christopher Parsons OBE, a former head of the BBC's Natural History Unit, once said, 'Filming nature was incredibly difficult; your subjects are too large or too small, too high in the air or hidden underground; their habitats are too dark, too cold, too hot, too wet or too dry; and none of them wanted to be on film anyway.'

It is also the most frustrating business. As Barry Paine says, 'When you arrive at the place where you're supposed to film, the rain's falling in sheets, the wind has reached gale force, you're soaked to the skin and there's no chance you'll take your camera out of its case, there is always somebody who seems to take great pleasure in telling you about the glorious weather that you just missed or the rare bird that's now gone.'

Another cameraman put it this way: 'You're waist deep in a muddy creek, you haven't slept for three days, what the mosquitoes haven't bitten the leeches and sweat bees are working on; the camera's playing up and you've just heard your partner has left you because they can't remember who you are!'

It is also a dangerous business and some have paid the ultimate price. German film cameraman Dieter Plage fell to his death from a miniature airship above the rainforest. The ultralite of 3-D large-format cameraman Noel Archambault from the USA crashed while filming in the Galapagos. Australian presenter Steve Irwin was stabbed in the chest by a stingray while delivering a piece to camera.

Others have come close to death. Alan Root has been charged at by a silverback mountain gorilla, was close to being killed by a hippo, has been bitten by a leopard and almost died from an allergic reaction to a puff-adder bite. Cameraman John Brown and researcher Stuart Armstrong walked away with minor injuries from a helicopter crash while filming for *British Isles: A Natural History* near Hadrian's Wall. And Doug Allan has twice been adrift on an ice floe in the Arctic with the prospect of rescue very much in the balance.

The first of these occasions was with producer Martha Holmes, when filming for *Wildlife Special: Polar Bear*. Accompanied by an Inuit guide, the two were on an ice floe which broke away from the main body of ice thanks to an off-course icebreaker and an unexpected blizzard. The helicopter that might have rescued them was grounded by the storm and the ice floe was drifting relentlessly towards open sea. Martha takes up the story:

'We put together a little shelter and had cups of tea. The guide was on the radio to his wife, and while all this was going on, I had this strange out-of-body experience. We were in this extraordinarily beautiful landscape, all white on white, and we had the prospect of dying. The storm was getting worse, and it was clear that our ice floe was getting smaller and smaller. Doug managed to get some sleep, which left me alone, and then after 20 hours when our situation looked bleak, the helicopter base [Resolute] came on the radio and said that it looked as if the storm was clearing. We were rescued not by a helicopter but by a small plane. The personnel came off first and the equipment came off on the second load. I went back on that flight and discovered that the ice floe had already broken in two. A few hours after that it would have gone altogether. It was a pretty close call.

'It was a life-changing scene. An instant death is horrific, but we had 20 hours to think about dying – how physically we were going to die – was I going to panic at the last minute? And then I thought, what an amazing place in which to go.'

Martha and Doug's experience is mercifully rare, but wildlife filmmaking is still a dangerous, uncomfortable and frustrating occupation. Yet people keep doing it. There is something about it that attracts people who want to share their enthusiasm for the *natural* world with the *whole* world. And it brings those magical moments when all the frustration, heartache and physical depredation are forgotten. For producer Miles Barton and cameraman Barrie Britton it was the time they became honorary babysitters to a nest of white-winged choughs.

'After ten days filming, they had got to know us so well they would leave the chicks, which had left the nest but couldn't fly, within a few feet of us while they went off to find food. They seemed to know that the chicks were safe with us.'

For others it is a moment of sheer beauty, as Keenan Smart recalls:

'One experience above all that I treasure is the one of sitting around a campfire in the African night, listening for those remarkable sounds – lions roaring, hyenas cackling, zebra stampeding – and the sense one has of going back to a primitive past, knowing that only a few hundred miles away Olduvai Gorge has all those fossils of early man. Somehow the eclipse of the moon, the fire and the sounds of the wildlife was extraordinary.'

Another source of wonder is a close encounter with animals that are teetering on the brink of extinction. When filming the Amur leopard for *Planet Earth* the film crew had not realized they were looking at a subspecies that would soon become extinct. There were estimated to be 46 in the wild at the time of filming, but a recent survey has dropped the estimate to between 27 and 35. Soon, the only way anyone will see an Amur leopard is either in a zoo or on a television film.

The archives of wildlife filmmakers contain images of animals that have already gone. In 1932, for example, film was taken of a Tasmanian tiger plodding around its bare cage. It was the last of its kind, and it died that same year. The species was lost, but we can still see how the animal looked and moved. In 1935, Arthur Allen filmed the ivory-billed woodpecker, a species long thought to be extinct, although there are more recent reports of isolated sightings. And the only place you will find Costa Rica's tiny golden toad, declared extinct in 1989, is in the NHU film vaults in Bristol.

So what of the future? Wildlife filmmaking is now a huge international industry, with dedicated film festivals serving as marketplaces where deals are done and ideas pitched. The 1978 International Wildlife Film Festival in Missoula was the first, and shortly afterwards, in 1982, the wildlife filmmaking community came together in Bristol for the first Wildscreen and the so-called 'green Oscars'.

At the time these festivals started, film was the preferred medium, but today High Definition (HD) is the buzzword. As with the arrival of colour, it takes viewers another step closer to reality. In *Natural World: Ant Attack*, for example, every hair on the ant's leg, indeed every hair on the mite on the ant's leg, is sharper than a pin and as the sun hits the damp rainforest floor the camera can pick out the tiniest droplets of water in the rising steam. HD also makes it easier to capture animals living in areas where the light is poor. Filming birds of paradise, for example, in their dark and dense rainforest home, was once exceedingly difficult, but HD cameras for *Planet Earth* captured extraordinary images of the blue bird of paradise. It was the first time its courtship ritual had been recorded on an electronic medium of any kind.

HD, though, is not a foolproof recipe for success. *Planet Earth* producer Huw Cordey discovered a shortcoming when filming wild camels in the Gobi Desert. The crew woke up early one morning to find blue skies, glistening snow but a temperature that had plummeted to –34°C (–30°F). There were no maps or roads and they had to find their way about by GPS, but eventually they tracked down their camel herd. Everything looked fine through the black-and-white viewfinders, but when they returned to camp they discovered that everything was a strong shade of yellow. The intense cold had knocked out the blue channel on the chip. The crew quickly learned to warm up the camera before starting to film.

In the long term, the broadcasting of natural history films could be supplanted by websites such as *Terra* and the children's equivalent *Terapod*, both mediated by the University of Montana, where viewers go not only to watch wildlife movies, but also to post their own films and videos. Video on demand will probably replace structured broadcasting schedules. But there will always be a need for some intrepid soul to go out there in the wilderness, to risk life and limb, to donate blood to leeches, ticks and mosquitoes, to be charged by rhinos and elephants, and to sit for hours in a cramped hide with nothing more than a bunch of sandflies for company, in order to bring back pictures of the overwhelming beauty and majesty of nature.

Wildlife filmmaking shall not die!

Martha Holmes and Mike de Gruy feeding butterfly fish in Hawaii during Sea Trek *filming.*

[CHAPTER ONE]

Pith Helmets and Penguins

On 29 August 1907, an audience at the Palace Theatre on the corner of London's Shaftesbury Avenue was mesmerized by moving images that had never been seen before. The theatre had been built in 1891 for Richard D'Oyly Carte as the Royal English Opera House – which was an abject failure – and just a year later it became the Palace Theatre of Varieties. But on this summer evening at the beginning of the twentieth century 'variety' encompassed 'nature', and for the first time a paying audience had the opportunity to watch British birds on the big screen. ☞

Above: The dummy bullock that the Kearton brothers used as a hide. Cherry Kearton was trapped inside for several hours before his brother freed him.

Early Pioneers

The event at the Palace Theatre was not the first 'animal' film. In 1896 American cinema pioneer Birt Acres, born of English parents, and Robert W. Paul had produced *The Boxing Kangaroo*, a film they made in Britain using camera equipment of Acres' own design (not to be confused with *Das Boxende Känguruh* made by Max Kladanowsky the previous year in Germany) and Louis Lumière had filmed a lion pacing up and down in London Zoo. It was not the first 'nature' film, for in 1895 Acres had recorded *Rough Sea at Dover*. It was also not the first 'scientific' film featuring animals, for Charles Durban's 1903 season of films at London's Alhambra Theatre with the umbrella title *The Unseen World* had featured extraordinary pioneering macrophotography with cheese mites (see Chapter Seven). It was, however, the first British 'wildlife' film, shot entirely on location.

The filmmaker was Oliver Gregory Pike. Born in Enfield, Middlesex, in 1877, he was to have quite an impact on the world of wildlife. In the late 1890s he became one of the first natural history stills photographers, even designing his own quarter-plate reflex camera – to be sold as 'The Birdland Camera' – and went on to become one of the pioneers of wildlife cinematography. His first wildlife film, and the one shown at the Palace that day in 1907, was *In Birdland*, a film about British birds. At least, we assume it was about British birds. The film was so popular in London that at least a hundred additional prints were made for distribution to theatres all over the country, yet not one survives; so the stars of the film must remain unknown and uncelebrated. The images would have been no more than 'moving stills pictures', a far cry from the action sequences and intimate encounters we see in wildlife films today, but they documented animal behaviour that had previously been witnessed and described by the privileged few, yet was now to be accessible to everyone.

In 1908, Oliver Pike became the first known filmmaker to visit St Kilda, the most westerly of the Outer Hebrides, 160 km (100 miles) off the Scottish mainland. He described it as a 'lost world' where the inhabitants spoke their own language and bartered without the use of money. It was to be 15 years before any other filmmaker ventured out to such an inaccessible spot, but Pike showed how he and others like him could operate in remote locations under potentially dangerous conditions. He filmed the islanders and the wildlife, including the enormous population of gannets that nested on St Kilda at that time. It was, perhaps, the dawn of a new awareness, stimulating the interest of a concerned and caring segment of the population that was one day to become the wildlife and conservation movement.

And that is the way it would have been from the outset, except that the showmen took over: enter Cherry Kearton, a farmer's son from Yorkshire. He and his elder brother Richard first went the way of Oliver Pike, taking stills of British wildlife, especially birds, and then tackling moving pictures. Cherry, however, took the genre one stage further, filming more elaborate sequences and starring in his own movies. He became the first wildlife celebrity.

Kearton was born in the Yorkshire village of Thwaite in Swaledale in 1871. His family house still stands beside the moorland he loved as a child. There are pictures of animals chiselled into the lintels above the main door, as well as his and Richard's birth dates in stones to either side. In an autobiographical cinema film, *The Big Game of Life* (1935), Cherry recalled the moment when the prospect of a farmer's life lost its appeal: 'Although I enjoyed this life, I grew restless and wanted to see the world. I had no concrete plans, but on the death of my father, when I was fourteen, I decided to go to London and, packing my simple belongings, I set out for the distant village of Hawes. I remember the mixture of joy and sorrow that filled me as I passed along the familiar road, perhaps never to return.'

A young Cherry Kearton up to his waist in water and acquiring an unavoidable chill.

When he reached the capital, he was probably most influenced by his brother. Richard Kearton was already an established wildlife stills photographer and Cherry joined him in his work, at that time for the publisher Cassells. Indeed, in 1895, the two brothers published a book of their photographs and experiences that became a bestseller. Cherry remembered the hardships they had to endure in order to obtain their groundbreaking photographs: 'To secure these pictures I stood neck deep in lakes, remained motionless for hours in treetops, disguised myself as a young forest and caught every variety of chills, but I got what I wanted.'

The Keartons adopted all manner of bizarre means to capture their subjects on film. They used giant tripods, one brother standing on the other's shoulders, to reach the viewfinder of a camera focused on a nest in a tree, or they clung to long ladders in order to photograph a bird on the highest branches. They had hides disguised as sheep or cattle, in which one or other would be incarcerated for hours on end. Cherry told of one occasion when his 'cow' fell over and somehow turned upside down, trapping him for several hours until his brother returned to let him out. It might have sounded like madness, but they were using methods to obtain pictures that had never been tried before.

Opposite: The Kearton brothers adopt an unusual stance while photographing a bird in its nest.

Far left: Cherry Kearton in a photographic hide.

Left: Cherry Kearton displays a legging which has been bitten through by a lion.

Into Africa

By the start of the twentieth century, Cherry, like Oliver Pike, had identified the new challenge of moving pictures. Richard failed to see the attraction. He gave up photography to become a successful writer and lecturer, leaving Cherry to plough his own furrow.

The younger Kearton invested in all the new technology. His camera was purchased from the Charles Urban Trading Company (see Chapter Seven) based in Rupert Street, off Piccadilly. It was made of mahogany and brass, and he painted it black to be less obtrusive in the wild. The lens was attached directly to the camera and could not be changed as lenses are today, although even then Cherry had telephoto lenses that enabled him to be some distance from the subject, yet appear closer than he really was.

The kit was extraordinarily cumbersome. He had to carry the huge camera, an equally enormous tripod, film, hide and any additional gear, probably to remote places so as to get away from people, and then, having set up all the equipment and settled down to wait for his subject, he had to hand-crank the camera. It was noisier even than a foot-operated sewing machine, scaring any self-respecting wildlife away. Today's film-makers acknowledge his skill. How he got anything, they say, was remarkable.

Cans of film discovered in the back rooms of London's Natural History Museum show Cherry Kearton crawling up to a buffalo and being charged by a rhino; it was all very gung-ho

Kearton's first subjects, like Pike's, were British birds – in fact, he was probably one of the first to capture them on film, working in a wood close to London in 1903. However, in 1909, a year after Pike was stalking the St Kildans, Kearton went one better. He went to Africa.

This was another first. He was going to places where no filmmaker had gone before, producing a wealth of material that was shown all around Britain. Right from the beginning his biggest star attraction was himself. He was seen crossing rivers with hastily erected rope bridges and riding horses across the East African savannah, but what must have been most dangerous was the filming of the wild animals themselves. He filmed elephants, hippos, rhinos, giraffes, zebras, wildebeest, lions and even dolphins off the bow of the ship on his outward journey. To do this, he needed to approach his subjects more closely than a modern cameraman would do, and he could not remain still. He or his assistant had to crank the camera with one hand, while panning and tilting with the other, so even the most short-sighted rhino could have spotted the white flash of his hands on the side of the camera and charged. Cans of film discovered in the back rooms of London's Natural History Museum show Kearton crawling up to a buffalo and being charged by a rhino; it was all very gung-ho.

Kearton's big break came when, in August 1909, he met former US president Theodore Roosevelt and filmed him on safari, although the film received mixed reviews. It was authentic and included footage of hippos in a lagoon, but it was thought to be less entertaining than a William N. Selig film of the same year, *Hunting Big Game in Africa,* that had been shot in a Chicago studio with a Roosevelt lookalike, African Americans as 'native porters' and an off-screen gunman who shot a lion bought from the local zoo! Roosevelt aside, Kearton's pictures were seen all over the world and when, in 1912, he signed a distribution deal in the USA his films were watched by millions. Worldwide book sales ensured that he became just as famous as his movies, an international superstar. His work, however, was beginning to raise questions. Filmmakers like Kearton were walking a precarious tightrope between science and entertainment, a delicate balance that is as challenging today as it was then.

In the USA, wildlife movies kicked off in 1897 with an Edison Manufacturing Company title, *The Sea Lion's Home*, which showed wild sea lions at the famous Golden Gate Park in San Francisco, lying on rocks and diving into the sea. A succession of films followed, featuring violent confrontations (*Fight Between Tarantula and Scorpion,*1900) or hunting (Pathé Frères' *Une Chasse à L'Ours Blanc,* released in the States as *Hunting the White Bear*, 1903). As on the British scene, potential celebrities were not shy about coming forward, the most notable being Martin and Osa Johnson.

Martin Johnson and Osa Leighty married in Kansas in 1910 and, after two trips in 1921 to film the 'cannibals' of the South Pacific, they embarked on an expedition to Kenya. They filmed what was described as the 'first purely commercial animal picture', a feature called *Trailing African Wild Animals* (1923) that played at New York's Capitol Theater. They were working with Carl Akeley, an animal collector and taxidermist who was the mastermind behind the dioramas in New York's American Museum of Natural History and the designer of a lightweight movie camera that could be used more easily on location. Their expedition had the backing and the blessing of the museum authorities.

The film itself purported to show a couple – the Johnsons – searching for and finding a lost lake – Lake Paradise – packed with wildlife that they had learned about through the diaries of a

Scottish missionary. Helen Bullit Lowry of the *New York Times Magazine* described it as 'a quest for the garden of Eden' and went so far as to praise the Johnsons for 'scientific accuracy', but the reality was quite different. The lake was well known to local Kenyans and to European traders, and sequences showing the Johnsons being stalked by lions and charged by rhinos were staged. Wildlife was generally cajoled into performing for the cameras by the three filmmakers.

Nevertheless, the film was a success and it led to others, such as *Simba* (1928), which took four years to complete and contains striking images of lions and other East African wildlife, ending with a lion hunt supposedly by Lumbwa warriors. A closer look shows that the sequence involved at least two quite separate events – footage the Johnsons took themselves of Lumbwa tribesmen and pictures of Masai hunters spliced in from another film by Alfred J. Klein. Some time later, George Eastman, one of the financial backers, revealed what actually happened.

Above and previous page: Film posters advertising work from the makers of the 'first purely commercial animal picture'.

The film crew had hired the Lumbwa and the crew's cars were used to drive the lions into an area suitable for filming and then corral them until the job was done. The public and the museum authorities were none the wiser, but a taste for Hollywood-style adventures meant that Martin and Osa Johnson went on to have a lucrative film career. In 1920, Swedish cameraman Oskar Olson filmed lions near the Mara River in East Africa, and the following year Carl Akeley and Herbert Bradley obtained the first film of gorillas in the eastern Congo (Akeley also killed them to be stuffed for a diorama in the African Hall at the American Museum of Natural History).

A Little Bit of Science

Others, meanwhile, were less flamboyant. In 1922, backed by amateur naturalist and wealthy factory owner Edgar Chance, Oliver Pike was asked to film a cuckoo laying its eggs in a meadow pipit's nest. He had already successfully filmed a cuckoo pushing a reed warbler chick out of the nest, but now he had a fresh challenge. The location was a common in Worcestershire and, in order to approach the nest, Pike, Chance and an entourage of interested friends and colleagues settled in hides disguised as bales of hay. The bales were scattered around the nest, almost surrounding it, so how the hen meadow pipit was not frightened away, let alone filmed, remains something of a mystery. Nevertheless, Pike was able to record the entire event. A naturalist as well as a filmmaker, he probably knew how to habituate his subject to the presence of the haystacks, gradually moving them forward until he was just 3.5 metres (12 feet) from the nest; and it paid off. Eventually, he filmed the cuckoo laying its eggs, the cuckoo hatchling tipping out the meadow pipit's eggs, and the pipit mother feeding the monstrous cuckoo chick – all in exquisite detail right in front of the camera.

Pike's cuckoo films were among the first examples of filmmakers casting new light on wild-animal behaviour, and it did not stop at that. Pike was using different-sized shots to tell his story, intercutting wides, medium shots and close-ups, beginning to create sequences rather than individual shots and introduce the grammar of filmmaking to wildlife films. *The Cuckoo's Secret* (1922) was the first in a series of 'shorts', each about ten minutes long, which preceded the main presentation in cinemas. The series was called *Secrets of Nature*, and it was so successful that it ran and ran until 1933.

Osa Johnson with ostrich eggs during the Johnsons's 1927–1928 Africa trip.

See Them, Hear Them

By the early 1930s another development was boosting the film industry – talkies – and wildlife filmmakers were soon cashing in on what was at first a novelty, but later became an integral part of the wildlife film. The *Secrets of Nature* series was quick off the mark with *Bath Time at the Zoo* (1929), followed by *Daily Dozen at the Zoo* (1930) and *Playtime at the Zoo* (1930). These films were modelled on Disney cartoons, with animal movements synchronized to music.

It was also in 1930 that Cherry Kearton made what was probably his most popular film, one in which he appears speaking to the camera. It was called *Dassan: An Adventure in Search of Laughter Featuring Nature's Greatest Little Comedians.* The 'little comedians' were penguins living on a small island off the southwest coast of South Africa. Kearton, ever the showman, dressed in pith helmet, khaki suit, gaiters and dark tie, is seen sitting smoking a pipe, standing and walking among literally millions of penguins – millions, according to Kearton, of 'Charlie Chaplins'. Even today, the sheer numbers take the breath away, so it must have been an extraordinary thing for cinema audiences to see at that time. However, Kearton did not stop at the natural spectacle. A line in the film – 'My story of penguin islands is of the strangest little creatures that bear a remarkable resemblance to human beings' – is the first warning shot, and when he introduces us to the penguins with 'I was then introduced to Frank and Flora Flatfeet, an affectionate young couple that were to act as my guides', you can guess how the rest of the film progressed. Comedy sounds, such as honky car horns, accompanied penguins on the move and they were assigned names like Riley and Ford. At one point, Kearton is seen waving his arms up and down as if trying to teach one clearly puzzled little character how to fly. It was more like a cartoon than a wildlife film and the 'little comedians' did not amuse many of Kearton's critics. His film career eventually fizzled out and he turned to books and radio. In 1940, he died on the steps of Broadcasting House, the BBC's headquarters in central London.

By this time Kearton's place in British wildlife filmmaking had been taken temporarily by a more heavyweight writer and presenter, the evolutionary biologist Julian Huxley. In 1934, Huxley collaborated with Welsh naturalist R.M. Lockley in the making of *The Private Life of the Gannets*, a documentary film directed by Alexander Korda. The birds were northern gannets, which conveniently (at least for the purposes of film distribution) live and breed on both sides of the Atlantic, and with the help of the Royal Navy they were filmed around Grassholm, off the Pembrokeshire coast. The film was released alongside Korda's 1934 feature *The Scarlet Pimpernel* and in 1937 it won an Oscar® for 'best short subject (one reel)'.

The following year, Huxley appeared in and supervised six short films with the title *The Animal Kingdom,* made by the Travel and Industrial Development Association of Great Britain (predecessor to the British Tourist Authority) in cooperation with the Zoological Society of London.

Scientists were quick to realize the potential of the research and educational films and many collaborations followed. Most notable titles in the non-theatrical market were *Ethology of the Greylag Goose* (1938), made in Britain by Nobel Prize-winning ethologist Konrad Lorenz, and in the USA *The Social Behaviour of the Laughing Gull* (1940), made by zoologist Gladwyn Kingsley Noble. Then came World War II and many wildlife filmmakers went to the front, their skills at working in often dangerous conditions well suited to capturing events on the battlefield.

In neutral Sweden, however, one filmmaker was able to continue his work throughout the war. Arne Sucksdorff was just 22 when he made his first documentary, and on its strength he was commissioned by Sweden's leading film studio, Svenska Filmindustri, to make a series of shorts about Swedish wildlife, including *A Summer's Tale* (1941), *Reindeer Time* (1943) and *Gull* (1944). Just after the war he took the wildlife film into pastures new with *The Shadow of the Hunter* (1947), about a hunter tracking a deer, and *Shadows on the Snow* (1949), with a tracker following a bear. In neither case were the animals shot, a new departure for hunting films. Instead, the films observed the behaviour of the animals closely, revealing their everyday struggle for survival; but there was humour and pathos, each sequence underlined by a flowing musical score. Some commentators believe that Sucksdorff's innovative filmmaking had taken him into the realms of Disney, some time before Disney embarked on wildlife filmmaking. The differences were that Sucksdorff's films were in black and white and he lacked the enormous Disney budgets and worldwide branding.

The Disney Phenomenon

How Walt Disney started in the wildlife business is not clear. Some say he became intrigued by the real wilderness when sketching the first scenes of his timeless animated feature *Bambi* (1942); others point to his holidays in Alaska. Whatever the reason, the Disney organization went into wildlife films in a big way with *True-Life Adventures*. The first of many shorts was *Seal Island* (1948), in which Disney harnessed the skills of amateur filmmakers Alfred and Elma Milote. The film won an Oscar® for best 'short subject (two reel)', and paved the way for features such as *The Living Desert* (1953), directed by James Algar, which followed a day in the life of creatures living in the deserts of the southwest USA. It picked up an armful of gongs, including an Academy Award®, a Golden Globe and an International Award at the Cannes Film Festival. It also marked a new departure for Disney. He had been having increasing problems getting his distributor RKO to take his *True-Life Adventures* seriously. 'Who's going to pay good money to watch creatures in a desert?' they said. As a consequence, Disney parted company with RKO and with his brother Roy set up the Buena Vista Distribution Company. *The Living Desert,* its first title, was made for half a million dollars and made $5 million on its first release. Disney had proved the film moguls wrong. Then came *The Vanishing Prairie* (1954), about the large animals that once roamed the American plains. It won another Oscar® – for Documentary (Feature) – and was highly praised the world over. The authenticity of the next Disney Academy Award® winner, however, was blighted by an overzealous cameraman.

Like its predecessors, Disney's *White Wilderness* (1958) was directed by James Algar and written and narrated by Winston Hibler. Its breathtaking visuals were greeted with universal praise. It was filmed over three years in Canada, but what the two veterans failed to notice was that one of the sequences was flawed. The cameraman, James R. Simon, filmed lemmings apparently committing mass suicide by leaping into the Arctic Ocean during their migration but, it turned out later, the entire event had been staged. It was filmed in Alberta, where there is no ocean and few lemmings. Simon purchased trapped lemmings from Inuit schoolchildren in Manitoba and filmed them from various angles to give the impression of large numbers. At the end of the sequence the unfortunate animals are attacked by gulls, ravens and a stoat before being herded over a crumbling cliff. Others race into the water across a shingle beach. As a result of many schoolchildren watching *White Wilderness*, the myth of lemming 'suicide' persists to this day and is an unfortunate black mark on an otherwise commendable film.

While Disney was putting wildlife film into cinemas, another revolution was taking place, this time on the small screen. In the USA in 1945, Marlin Perkins, the director of Lincoln Park Zoo in Chicago, was taking animals into the television studio at WBKB for shows like *Zoo Parade*. On one occasion during rehearsals Perkins was bitten by a timber rattlesnake, but he survived and went on to front such long-running shows as *Mutual of Omaha's Wild Kingdom* (1963–88). *Zoo Parade* was a local show; the first to be distributed across the USA was *Fishing and Hunting Club* in 1949. On the other side of the Atlantic, wildlife filmmaking for television was stirring too, but its origins were quite different.

MOVING STILLS

The origins of wildlife filmmaking can be traced to the pioneering days of the motion-picture industry. It all began as a wager, or so legend would have it. In 1877, English-born photographer Eadweard Muybridge (1830–1904) was experimenting with multiple cameras to capture motion when he was approached by soon-to-be governor of California, Leland Stanford, to settle a $25,000 bet: whether a racehorse in full gallop actually left the ground completely and 'flew' through the air. Muybridge's photograph proved that all four hooves were free of the ground at the same moment, but he was inspired to take the matter further. The following year, he photographed a galloping horse using not one but 50 cameras. He chose a dark horse, fitted out the jockey with dark clothes and had them run against a white wall on a bright sunny day for the greatest contrast. The horse ran through a series of trip wires, each wire triggering the shutter of a camera. The result was a series of stills.

Muybridge photographed a horse using cameras with shutters set to a speed of 1/500 second and then released by threads broken by the horse or by clockwork.

In 1882, the photographs were published by J.B.D. Stilman, an associate of Stanford, in *The Horse in Motion*. He realized that the photographs could be placed on separate pages, one after the other, and then flipped like a flipbook. It was the first experience of moving pictures and the precursor to motion pictures proper. Muybridge, in fact, invented a moving picture system, the zoopraxiscope, which was similar to the zoetrope (a cylinder with slits cut in it) but was able to project images so that an entire audience could see people or animals moving at the same time.

[CHAPTER TWO]

Mother Meets Auntie

Mother Nature first met 'Auntie' BBC on radio, on a station known then as the Home Service, the forerunner of Radio 4. Just after the end of World War II, television was in its infancy, with just one channel in the UK – the BBC – and, in a tradition it has maintained to this day, the organization was reorganizing. This time it was devolving programme-making departments to the regions. Birmingham inherited agriculture, Manchester was strong on variety and the music hall, but the West Region had the managers scratching their heads. What could Bristol do? The answer came from a young radio features producer who moved to Bristol from London in 1946. ☞

Above: A young David Attenborough tests sound recording equipment in the Georgetown Botanic Gardens, Guyana, for Zoo Quest.

James Fisher (right) with Bob Veeraswamy and a tree porcupine in an early outside broadcast from Paignton Zoo.

Exploding Tortoises

It was Desmond Hawkins who, in 1946, suggested that Bristol should host 'countryside programmes'. He recalled the mood at the time: 'What I had to do was see what our assets were. We realized we didn't have major sport – there was never a test match or an international game of soccer in the West Country. We didn't have big light entertainment, that was in London or Blackpool, but what we did have was rather attractive countryside – romantic countryside really – the kind of countryside people want to visit, and so that was something I thought we should try to develop; and they decided they would take a reckless gamble and commission three programmes, and we'll see what happens after that.'

So it came to pass that countryside and nature became Bristol's speciality. Hawkins developed *The Naturalist* (1946), the first natural history programme on radio, and followed it with *Bird Song of the Month* (1947), *Out of Doors* (1948) and *Birds in Britain* (1951). Listeners were glued to their wireless every Sunday afternoon after the one o'clock news bulletin to listen to *The Naturalist*, and such notable naturalists as Maxwell Knight and James Fisher were introduced to the listening public.

'People really had it up to their chins with muck and filth, misery, worry, anxiety and death and destruction,' Hawkins remembered. 'There was a wish to find a paradise lost, and this was the appeal of the wild to those first audiences in the late Forties, early Fifties. In radio, you had for the first time the ability to take people to the actual sound of nature through sound recordings.'

Most of the early programmes were live and the recordings were played in from wax discs. Hawkins told of one occasion when things did not go quite to plan:

'One thing I was very eager to record was the sound of the Severn Bore, and we met at Minsterworth on the day of the highest tides. We were in plenty of time to get ready and had been assigned a BBC engineer, who came with a brand-new recording van. Being so new, every single part of it was wrapped in greaseproof paper, so it all had to be unwrapped and assembled … and he was not the most rapid of workers. I began to get worried as time went on … but he said everything would be fine, he'd be ready when the moment came.

'So I went down the bank holding a microphone, waiting for the bore to come along. It might be eight feet higher than the water it's passing over, so it whooshes up the bank and you could be swept away, so we had a chain of hands, involving local farmers, one holding my hand, another holding his and so on right the way back. They thought that way they wouldn't see me floating all the way up to Gloucester. So we waited.

'Sure enough, just as people had described it, it was a noise like an express train approaching – a tremendous roaring noise – and then round the bend it came, quite frightening when you see it. It went past, a wonderfully dramatic experience. I was soaked from head to foot, but triumphant. The chaps pulled me back up and all seemed well. Then something strange happened. I hadn't realized you could talk back in reverse through a microphone, and to my astonishment the microphone I was holding in my hand suddenly emitted a voice, which I recognized as the engineer's, saying firmly and clearly, "I'm ready now!"'

HAWKINS, *BIRDSONG OF THE MONTH*

'There was a wish to find a paradise lost, and this was the appeal of the wild to those first audiences in the late Forties, early Fifties.

Hawkins eventually did get that recording of the Severn Bore and it joined the many new recordings being made daily by early wildlife sound recordists, including the German naturalist Ludwig Koch, who bequeathed his entire collection to the BBC. It was the basis of Bristol's sound library, one of the biggest in the world, and some of Koch's original recordings are still in use today.

Long-running series such as *The Living World* and *Wildlife Questions* followed. Both programmes were introduced originally by the incomparable Derek Jones, who never missed an edition in all the years he was in the chair. *Wildlife Questions* was one of the first natural history programmes to involve the audience. Each week, the office was deluged with letters from listeners asking their questions about both

British and exotic wildlife. Sometimes they sent in specimens, so it was always with some trepidation that the programme assistants opened Monday morning's post – it often contained a matchbox or two with live spiders, beetles or flies inside. Many times, the specimen had turned to an unpleasant mush, including a mouse that was probably freshly dead when it was sent but had become an evil-smelling soup by the time it arrived. Heaven knows how it came through the post-office sorting system. The post boy brought it on the end of a stick!

WILDLIFE QUESTIONS

The questions were sometimes strange, too. There was, for example, the man who wrote in to tell the programme that his tortoise had exploded.

The questions were sometimes strange, too. There was, for example, the man who wrote in to tell the programme that his tortoise had exploded. Absurd as this may sound, when the *Wildlife Questions* panel of four naturalists examined the evidence it became clear that the tortoise had died while in hibernation and that the activity of bacteria had caused it to ferment and explode. Then there was the question asking whether bees were left- or right-handed, another about whether snails shrieked and one from a child wanting to know where bees went to the toilet. Intriguing and thought-provoking, such questions always raised entertaining and informative answers from the panel.

LOUD AND CLEAR

In the more recent past, *The Natural History Programme* joined the ranks of radio programmes from Bristol, presented first by Fergus Keeling and Lionel Kellaway. Lionel had cut his teeth on programmes for BBC Wales and remembered a bit of advice he was given there that later stood him in good stead:

'One way of putting contributors at ease is the use of their Christian name. Having been told this by an experienced broadcaster, I turned up at an interview and introduced myself. I'd already talked to the chap, a South Wales gamekeeper, on the telephone to get some background and tell him what we wanted to do, so I greeted him with, "Hello Bob, nice to see you, lovely day," and then, "Right, Bob, this is what we're going to do," and so on throughout the interview, starting most questions with "Bob". We had a wonderful interview. He had been a bit nervous at first, but he'd warmed up, so I said to him, "Well, Bob, that wasn't too bad, was it?" And he said, "Oh, I really enjoyed that, but if you don't mind me saying so, my name's not Bob, it's Harry."'

Of course, interviewers on location – whether on radio or television – not only need to know the interviewee's name, ask the questions and listen to the answers, they also have to worry about the traffic or whether an aircraft is flying overhead. One rookie radio producer became obsessed with acoustics. She had been told by the senior producer to choose a room with as little echo as possible and as it was her first interview she wanted to get it right. The interviewee was a man who had made a butterfly map of London and the two started the interview in his kitchen. The producer thought it was not quite right, so she tried the garden, but there were dogs barking everywhere. She tried his drawing room and that was not right, so he said, 'What about the bedroom?' So she said, 'That sounds a good idea', thinking that there would be a lot of padding in there, and they went upstairs. She was still unhappy with the acoustics and was admitting to herself that she must have been absolutely mad when she heard him say, 'What about under the duvet?'

She was, of course, thinking totally about the quality of the sound, so they actually did the interview under the duvet and got a good recording. It did, however, dawn on her that this was not the best situation to be in, so she finished the interview quickly, said a hasty 'Goodbye' and ran off down the street as fast as her legs would carry her.

Lionel Kellaway, by then an experienced interviewer who made sure he had the interviewee's name right, was still not immune to the bane of actors, presenters and interviewers everywhere – uncontrolled laughter or 'corpsing'.

'We were doing an interview soon after many beaches had been condemned in a European report on sewage pollution. I went to see a scientist at a university who was carrying out research on sewage pollution. We were going through all the different types of pollution and where it came from, and he was rather a straight chap, a little "correct", a little pompous and a little bit apprehensive about the interview. This often induces a sort of "stuffed-shirted-ness", so he was sitting back behind his desk, saying, "Well, there are several sorts of sewage pollution" and he listed one or two of them and then he said, "Of course, the sewage here is macerated sewage, it's chopped up into lots of little pieces, but where they don't have these new screens, we get an awful lot of what we call in the trade unacceptable floatables." At that point, I found it funny enough, but the producer who was holding the microphone started shaking and I glanced out of the corner of my eye, and it got worse and worse, until she was convulsing and purple with stifled laughter, and then she just corpsed with uncontrollable fits and giggles, and of course I caught it. So we had to stop, go away and have a cup of tea, calm down and come back and try again … We tried three times before we could stop laughing.'

In the early 1950s natural history radio was the 'senior service' in BBC West Region's network programmes. Things, however, were beginning to stir in television.

Peter Scott feeds a group of ducks and geese at Slimbridge while Desmond Hawkins looks on during a recording of The Naturalist *in December 1947.*

Birdwatchers and Television

While the countryside programme makers gathered in Bristol, the ornithologist Peter Scott was setting up the Severn Wildfowl Trust (now the Wildfowl and Wetlands Trust) at Slimbridge in Gloucestershire, a few miles to the north of Bristol. His father, Captain Robert Falcon Scott, had written to his mother during his fateful expedition across Antarctica, 'Make the boy interested in natural history; it is better than games, which they teach at some schools.' At first Peter Scott, like many of his day, was more interested in shooting wildlife. He was an enthusiastic wildfowler, but one day at Slimbridge he found a female goose that had been shot and was lying injured on the sands. Her mate stood by her for many hours and there and then Scott decided he would shoot guns no more. Instead, he set up one of the first nationwide conservation organizations. Desmond Hawkins remembered their first meeting:

'Peter Scott was a fine artist, he'd raced in the Olympics in sail boats, won European ballroom championships and won gliding competitions. I thought he really had more talent than was healthy for one man to have. However, he'd become interested in white-fronted geese on the river Severn. When I went over to look at them, I found my way blocked by a large shooting brake with a man in a duffle coat leaning over it. He had a telescope and was looking at the geese. I said to him, "I think you must be Peter Scott."

"'Yes," he said, "I am, and you're very lucky, because if you take my telescope you will see only the seventh lesser white-fronted goose ever to be recorded in the British Isles."

'And that was really a good foundation for what became a great friendship.'

Hawkins took an interest in a series of lectures Scott was presenting to schools, natural history clubs and even town halls, where he lectured to one thousand or two thousand people, and went along to one. Scott did quick sketches of birds and presented short pieces of film he had made, and this was the seed for what followed. When television caught up with wildlife in the early 1950s, it is no coincidence that the first natural history programme on British television was a live outside broadcast from Slimbridge – *Severn Wildfowl,* presented by Peter Scott in May 1953.

In December, several programmes followed, usually broadcast late on Saturday evenings, with the title *Wild Geese*. The studio was at first at Lime Grove in London, but eventually an outside broadcast mobile-control vehicle that could be permanently sited at Bristol became available and a makeshift TV studio was hastily put together so that the programmes could be made there. The programmes were mainly about Scott's own expeditions in Iceland, Greenland and South America. He had seen the benefits of showing films at fund-raising events for his budding wildfowl trust. Other contributions came from the likes of artist and ornithologist Roger Tory Peterson, mammal expert Ernest Neal and birdwatching enthusiast and distinguished soldier Viscount Alanbrooke.

The programmes had their origins in radio and at first relied very much on the spoken word, interspersed with short pieces of film. For one thing, television cameras were enormous and exceedingly cumbersome, and very few people were using cine cameras, so technology dictated what could and could not be achieved. So these early shows tended to give other people's interpretation of natural events rather than enabling the audience to witness them for itself.

On the other side of the country, meanwhile, the Royal Society for the Protection of Birds (RSPB) started to film British birds for its lecture circuit, part of an awareness programme aimed at conserving birds and their habitats. In 1953 George Edwards was tasked with setting up its one-man film unit. He already had films to his credit, such as *Birds of a Country Estate* (1951), about two Welsh estates, Llysdinam and Doldowlod, and the RSPB had commissioned a colour film about the Minsmere and Havergate reserves the year before. By 1956, the society was ready for its first get-together at the Royal Festival Hall on London's South Bank. It was the première of *Birds of Britain* and thereafter the film show became an annual event, with new films added each year to a rapidly building catalogue.

AN ACE IN THE HAND

By the start of 1955, Peter Scott's occasional programmes from Bristol were attracting significant attention, but nobody was prepared for the furore sparked by the arrival of German naturalist and filmmaker Heinz Sielmann in January that year. Scott had seen Sielmann lecturing at the International Ornithological Congress at Basel, Switzerland, when scouting for films for his television programme. Sielmann had made his first (silent) wildlife film, *Birds of Shore and Meadow*, in 1938, and after the war had built up a considerable track record, but it was his film on woodpeckers that had the nation buzzing. Sielmann had placed a camera in the back of a woodpecker's nest so that, for the first time, the viewing audience could witness all the comings and goings of the parents and the rearing of the chicks. It was sensational. Ecstatic viewers blocked the BBC's telephone lines for two hours after the broadcast. It was then that the BBC realized how important natural history programmes would be to its schedules.

'It put an ace in my hand,' Desmond Hawkins recalled. 'There was no way they were going to stop us after that.'

Indeed, nothing did stop them, for wildlife programmes were by now among the most popular on British television. By September 1955, Peter Scott was fronting a weekly programme, *Look*. It followed a familiar format of studio-based links and conversations introducing wildlife films, of which the first was another Heinz Sielmann contribution, this time on foxes. More films and more animals followed, and the following year the series launched with a film on whales, followed by items from Spain, Kenya and Scotland. The run also included a rather brave edition that enabled viewers to look down a microscope and see pond life 'live'.

Above: HRH The Duke of Edinburgh was Peter Scott's guest in a special 'Living with Nature' edition of Look *in 1966.*

Opposite: Peter Scott films marine iguanas in the Galapagos Islands for Faraway Look *with the Kodak cinecamera he used to collect material for his lectures.*

Scott ad-libbed most of his presentations. He rarely learned his lines. In his own words, he just 'got out there and did it'. The programmes were 30 minutes long, with about eight minutes of film. The rest was discussion, interviews, models and sketches drawn by Scott; in fact, as Hawkins put it, 'anything you could think of'. The problem was that in those days there were no staff cameramen and very few outside with the necessary skills. Amateur filmmakers were at a premium.

Naturalist and broadcaster Tony Soper was in there right at the beginning. Starting with the BBC in Plymouth, he managed to get himself posted to Bristol and became the *Look* producer. One of his tasks was to find film for each programme and he would call Peter Scott's friends and anyone else he could track down who had a film camera and did bird films in their holidays.

In the television retrospective *Wildlife Jubilee* (1982), Peter Scott and Tony Soper celebrated the era of the amateur filmmaker and acknowledged how vital these people had been. Naturalists like H.G. Hurrell in South Devon and Eric Ashby in the New Forest had made wonderful films, but they had other jobs. Nevertheless, Soper reckoned that they were dedicated to, and completely at home with, their subjects.

Wildlife filmmaker Eric Ashby and his home-made camera 'blimp', filming near a badger set.

'You can call him amateur, if you like,' he said of Eric Ashby, 'but by the time you put him through the editing and production process, I think his material is as good as anyone's. The reason is that he's spent a great deal of time setting things up, and his animals are real and wild. He may wait a week for them to turn up, but when they come they are real wild foxes looking for trouble and being careful, whereas a lot of wildlife film nowadays is made in controlled conditions.'

Tony was referring here to filming animals in 'sets', which were built much like a set for, say, a costume drama, but often in miniature. They enabled the camera operator to obtain big close-ups of eyes, of noses and ears twitching, of small animals that would quickly run away and of behaviour that would be impossible to capture in the wild because animals are so nervous. Eric Ashby, though, would have none of that. He filmed everything out there in the wild and dreamed up new ways of getting those must-have close-ups. In a film on foxes, he found it relatively easy to film cubs playing, but when they grew, they became more wary.

'The trouble was the noise of the camera,' he once recounted, 'and the only way to smother that was to put it in a box stuffed with soundproofing.'

Ashby invented a 'blimp'. It may have looked Heath Robinson, but it worked and he had wild foxes and other British wildlife behaving quite naturally in front of

Eric Ashby constructs a foxes den in 1973 – his elaborate sets enabled cameras to capture animals behaving naturally in their environment

his camera, including the marvellous sequence of badgers emerging from their den, sitting upright on their haunches and scratching … and scratching … and scratching, one of the funniest natural moments in wild film history.

It was films like these that saw a shift in emphasis from disseminating 'knowledge' to 'entertaining' with a small 'e'. Desmond Hawkins saw the importance of satisfying the broader audience:

'Having, as it were, gone for knowledge, what you must not do is to destroy the wonder, the excitement, the glamour and the joy of the subject. If you are going to go for a mass audience and the excitement of working in the mass media, you must take a subject and say, I am going to go out and interest not just a few hundred people who share my interest, I am going to talk to millions of people who have never thought about this and I am going to interest them as they have never been interested before.'

A Landmark Year

By 1957, *Look* was well established as a prime-time delight, but until then television had been very much the poor relation of radio. The *Radio Times* of 15 February, however, marked a big change. Previously, the television listings had been tucked away at the back of the magazine, after radio, but now they were switched to the front. ITV had been launched in September 1955 and after 18 months was gaining ground on the BBC mighty fast. ITV producers had already been sniffing around the Institut fur Film und Bild, for which Heinz Sielmann had made his films, but Desmond Hawkins had agreed an exclusive broadcast deal on behalf of the BBC.

Above: Charles Lagus filming baby coati with Kodak Cine Special in Guyana, 1955.

Opposite: Charles Lagus filming in the forests of the Upper Mazaruni Basin, Guyana.

The year 1957 also had great significance for wildlife filmmaking generally. In February Frank Gillard, the West Region's controller and former war correspondent, sent a memorandum to London headed 'BBC Natural History Unit'. It was the culmination of a report by Desmond Hawkins, endless meetings in London and many visits from BBC dignitaries to Bristol. Then, in April, the BBC's Board of Governors (replaced today by the BBC Trust) met in Bristol. They decided unanimously that the small group of people from the West Region who were involved in natural history programming should be recognized as a 'unit', and the NHU was born.

It was an unusual unit in BBC terms in that it kept radio and television together – what Hawkins used to call an 'ambidexterity', and a relationship that exists to this day. Its first head was Nicholas Crocker, though the position had initially been offered to a young, London-based producer called David Attenborough, who had

made his name in a series of studio-based programmes with Sir Julian Huxley called *The Pattern of Animals*. Attenborough then met Jack Lester, curator of reptiles at London Zoo, who was interested in his suggestion that the BBC accompany him on a quest for an especially rare bird. Attenborough asked Lester what it was called and he replied, 'The bald-headed rock crow'; not the catchiest of titles, thought Attenborough, so they simply called the series *Zoo Quest*.

After the first expedition – to Sierra Leone in 1954 – Lester fell ill and ended up in the London School for Tropical Medicine. However, the show had to go on and a new head of department, Leonard Miall, suggested that Attenborough should take Lester's place to present the programmes as well as produce them. And so a living legend was born.

Over the next ten years *Zoo Quest* went to such exotic places as Indonesia in the quest for a Komodo dragon, and to British Guiana, New Guinea, Paraguay and Madagascar. The series' cameraman, Charles Lagus, was one of the first to use 16mm film in a clockwork camera that ran for no more than 15 to 20 seconds at a time. At that time, 35mm film was the only acceptable format, but the cameras were large. Attenborough and Lagus wanted to be more mobile, so they opted for 16mm. The counter-argument was that 35mm was the 'professional' standard, but after an exchange of memos and a stormy meeting the Head of Film Department backed down, but not before stating very publicly, 'If 16mm is introduced as standard practice to BBC Television, it will be over my dead body.'

ZOO QUEST

Travel in those days was much less straightforward than today and once a film crew reached a distant country they had to stay for three or four months.

FARAWAY FILMING

Travel in those days was much less straightforward than today and once a film crew reached a distant country they had to stay for three or four months. They had little money for research, so they would arrive in, say, Borneo, find a canoe and paddle off into the interior in the hope of running into something worth filming. In these remote places, there was, of course, no way of communicating with the outside world. David Attenborough recalls one time in Indonesia when Charles Lagus wanted news of his newborn baby. They went to Java, booked a call to London and had to wait four days for it to come through (it was a girl, incidentally).

This also meant the crew had little feedback about the footage they were obtaining. If there was some mistake or malfunction in the camera, for example, they might be working for a couple of months without knowing that anything was wrong. Attenborough recalls one occasion in Borneo, three days' journey by river from the coast, when they were staying in a longhouse with the Dayak people. Attenborough was sitting on the veranda overlooking the river when he saw someone feverishly paddling a canoe towards him.

'To my surprise,' he remembers, 'the canoeist came to the bank just by the village and ran up to the longhouse. He was holding a stick and at the end of this stick was a piece of paper. I realized this was the original "cleft stick". The message was from London and it said, "Recent research has revealed imperative use reflector with all colour shots," but there was no way I was going to get a reflector. It would

Radio 4 presenters Fergus Keeling and Lionel Kellaway enjoying the recording of The Natural History Programme.

have been five days' journey at the end of which I might have found a reflector, so even after all this trouble all one could do was roll up the paper and throw it back in the river!'

With several series of *Zoo Quest* behind him, Attenborough was asked to consider a move to Bristol to lead the new unit, but with his family in London and his children established in schools in Richmond, he was reluctant to leave the capital. And anyway, he already had a decent job and his prospects looked good …

During those early days, where to get the next piece of film around which to base a wildlife programme was always a pressing problem. One solution was to follow Peter Scott's travels. In 1956, he was an official at the Melbourne Olympics, so the BBC enlisted the help of Charles Lagus and an overseas spin-off from *Look*, called *Faraway Look*, was created. Peter Scott's adventures in Australia, New Zealand and New Guinea duly graced the summer schedules.

Tony Soper filming grey seals with a long focal length lens, Pembrokeshire, UK.

The availability of a film had always dictated whether a subject was tackled on television, but that was about to change. The NHU had to take the initiative and Tony Soper was quick to respond. He went down the road with some petty cash to Dunscombe's, an optician's shop in Bristol that sold cameras, bought a second-hand Bolex and travelled to the Fair Isles, between Shetland and Orkney, to film seabirds. When *Look* number 41 hit the airways in 1958, it was with James Fisher introducing Tony's film *The Fulmar*.

After that, there was no stopping him. The following year, Tony and Peter Scott headed to the British Virgin Islands and the Galapagos for another series of *Faraway Look*. This time the films were being made not by an outside practitioner but by one of the NHU's own staff, and this was just the start. The idea for the NHU's first colour film, *The Major* (1963), produced by Christopher Parsons and showing the last days of an oak tree on a village green, sprang up from within the unit, an enormous breakthrough. It was to set the pattern for the way wildlife films in the BBC are made to this day.

THE DAWN OF 16MM

UNTIL THE MID-1950s all the BBC's professionally made films were shot on 35mm cameras, but by the time *Zoo Quest* was commissioned, cameraman Charles Lagus and producer David Attenborough were among the growing number who felt that 16mm cameras, being lighter and more flexible, would be more suitable for wildlife subjects. They approached the head of film operations for support. 'Over my dead body,' was the reply. The problem was that 16mm was viewed as a sub-standard format aimed at amateurs. During the 1950s and 1960s, however, the BBC worked extensively with Kodak to bring 16mm to a professional level. It eventually became the television industry standard, followed in the 1980s by Super 16, with a larger frame in a widescreen format to coincide with the arrival of widescreen television sets.

Charles Lagus films driver ants with a 16mm camera in Sierra Leone in 1954.

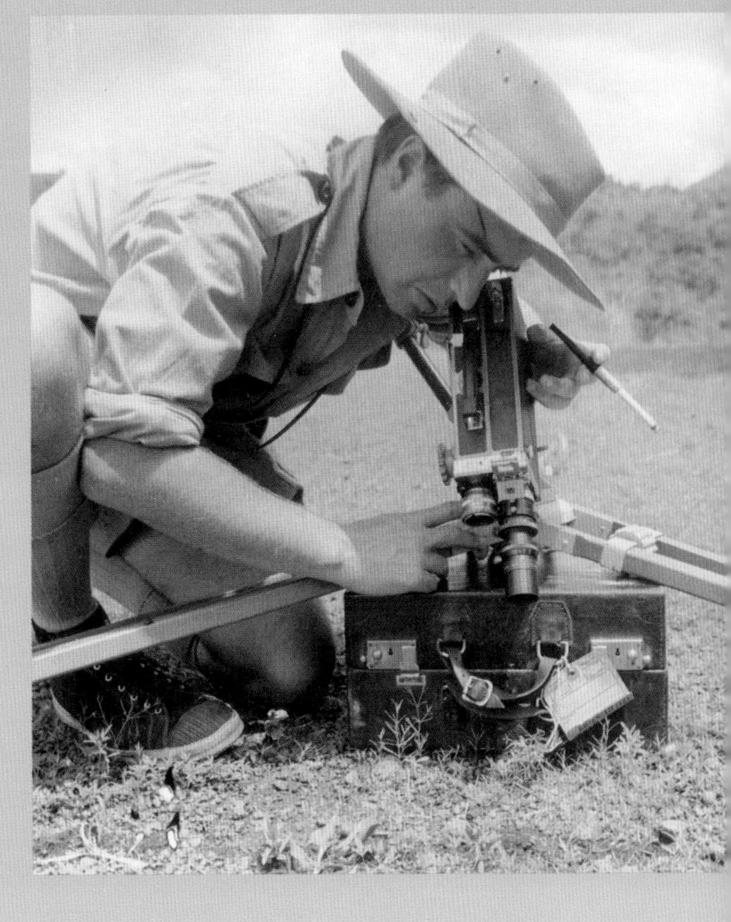

In those early days, the cameras such as Bolex and Beaulieu, were clockwork, a single wind giving no more than 15–20 seconds of film time at the normal speed of 24 frames per second. Later, electronic versions were developed, with names such as Arriflex and Aarton appearing on equipment lists. These cameras could run at up to 150 frames per second, which when played back at normal speed could slow the frantic flapping of bird flight or the erratic movements of insects to a point at which they appeared smoother or more elegant. Photosonics even had a camera that ran at a staggering 10,000 frames per second, giving wildlife filmmakers the ability to show, for the first time, exceedingly fast events such as the strike of a cobra or the lightning tongue of a chameleon.

Today, film is beginning to take a back seat. High-definition video is set to become the format that best captures the natural world.

[CHAPTER THREE]

Coming of Age

While names like Cherry Kearton in the UK and Martin and Osa Johnson in the USA dominated in the early days of wildlife filmmaking, in the late 1950s the British television audience was introduced to a whole new gamut of budding celebrities, including several husband-and-wife teams. In 1955 Hans and Lotte Hass took us *Diving to Adventure* (see chapter eight); three years later Armand and Michaela Denis invited us to join them *On Safari* in East Africa. ☞

Above: Underwater explorers Hans and Lotte Hass prepare to go Diving to Adventure.

A Distinguished Couple

Although not well known to the public, the Denises had first appeared on British television in October 1953. In 1954 made their first series for the BBC, *Filming Wild Animals,* a combination of studio presentation and filmed inserts from Tsavo National Park, Kenya, in which they caught a baby elephant, showed stick insects and scorpions, and Michaela danced with the Wakamba tribe.

Armand Denis became an influential character in the wildlife filming community, specializing in documentaries made in Africa. By the time his films reached the BBC, he had an impressive collection of cameramen working with him – Alan Root, Hugo van Lawick and Des Bartlett, to name but a few, all of whom became leading filmmakers in their own right. The NHU inherited his programmes from London, the argument being that wildlife was now Bristol's responsibility, but the fledgling NHU producers were nervous about the way the programmes were made. For one thing, Armand made an enormous number of films and the title sequence always showed him standing proudly with his movie camera in hand, but he and Michaela were often not directly involved with the events depicted on the screen. The designated cameraman (usually a man, by the way, for there were few camerawomen at that time) would film in a particular area and then Armand and Michaela would appear at camp. They performed their pieces to camera, such as the search for Gertie, the rhino with the strangely curved horn, or a 'pet in the warden's garden' that Michaela would meet, and then move on.

Above and opposite: Armand and Michaela Denis go On Safari.

Armand Denis, though, had a vision for the future. He insisted on filming everything in colour, even though the BBC would only pay for black and white. 'There will be colour television very soon,' he said, 'so I will pay the difference and shoot in colour,' and he was right. He was also quite shrewd. His contract with the BBC was for black and white films. With the coming of colour, he was able to negotiate with them all over again.

On Safari ran until the mid-1960s, when two major advances hit UK television – colour and BBC2. The second controller of the new channel (the first's reign was

short-lived) was David Attenborough, who was quick to realize the potential of 'landmark' television series with such epics as Kenneth Clark's *Civilisation* (1969) and Jacob Bronowski's *Ascent of Man* (1973). He also saw the importance of nature, travel and anthropology. Colour brought wildlife films and their audience one step closer to nature. And the creation of a second BBC channel broke another strait-jacket. Until then, most programmes had been no more than 30 minutes long. Now came an opportunity to make longer films, and in 1968 *The World About Us* was born, with a brief to provide more in-depth studies of particular places, plants or animals. It ran for 25 years and under its umbrella even the less glamorous creatures took on a new lease of life. Plankton, care of macro- and microphotography specialist Peter Parks and his 'optical bench', were as full of wonder and interest in *The Living Sea* as, say, the private life of the grizzly bear in Yellowstone National Park in *Grizzly*.

Storytellers and Moneymakers

These developments also meant that wildlife filmmaking had to be more sophisticated as a genre. In the early 1960s, filmmakers could go out and film virtually any living thing and almost guarantee it had not been filmed before, so they could get away with the sheer novelty of it. By the end of the decade, however, that approach was no longer tenable: films had to tell a story. This brought to the fore a whole new breed of wildlife filmmakers, who were experimenting with novel ways of gathering pictures.

One of the first in a long line of talented British filmmakers to emerge at this time was Ron Eastman, whose remarkable footage of a kingfisher diving to catch fish, taken from the fish's point of view, shot him into the public eye. 'Whatever Sielmann could do,' claimed Desmond Hawkins, 'he could do, and he picked on one of the most difficult birds you could imagine – a rare bird, difficult to get close to or to study easily and, like Sielmann's woodpecker, it has its young hidden away in a hole, not in a tree but in a bank – even worse!' In 1967 Eastman's *The Private Life of the Kingfisher* became the BBC's first natural history film to be broadcast in colour. It was *Look* number 144.

LOOK NO. 144

In 1967 Eastman's The Private Life of the Kingfisher *became the BBC's first natural history film to be broadcast in colour.*

In *Mzima: Portrait of a Spring*, an early production for *The World About Us*, Alan and Joan Root devised all sorts of ways to film wildlife under water, from a glass-fronted punt to a thinly disguised under water hide. It was the first time that hippos and crocodiles had been seen below the surface. It was also the time when an angry hippo nearly cost them their lives. Root and Joan were filming under water when the hippo lunged at them, its tooth tearing into the side of Joan's face mask. She was inches from a serious injury, even death. It was just one of many such incidents in the never-a-dull-moment career of these particularly intrepid filmmakers.

Hugo van Lawick and Jane Goodall on the shores of Lake Tanganyika at Gombe Stream National Park.

Hugo van Lawick brought us *Jane Goodall and Her Wild Chimpanzees* in the *Life* series, a natural history magazine about conservation and ecology presented by Desmond Morris on BBC2, while on *The World About Us* his film about *The Wild Dogs of Africa* had the entire nation transfixed by a wild puppy he called Solo.

In *Namib: Strange Creatures of the Skeleton Coast,* Jen and Des Bartlett filmed spiders that turned cartwheels, beetles that stood on their heads to drink, golden moles hunting beneath the sand, a lizard with hot feet and the staggeringly beautiful scenery of the coastal desert breaking through the fog.

The BBC, however, was by now far from being the only player on the world stage. On ITV, it was the East Anglia franchise that took an interest in wildlife films, its genesis remarkably similar to the BBC's. In 1960, Aubrey Buxton (later Lord Buxton) had developed the local Anglia Television series *Countryman*, sowing the seed of a more ambitious strand of programmes called *Survival* that was to put Survival Anglia among the leading production companies making wildlife films. Its first edition, *The London Scene* (1961), found Buxton himself driving around the capital in a vintage Bentley, filming such gems as urban foxes raiding dustbins. The strand, however, was different from the BBC's output in that it had to generate advertising revenue. It was Survival Anglia, then, that first explored the prospects of international co-production and collaboration. It went on to support Alan Root's *Enchanted Isle* (1968), the first British-made wildlife film to be aired on US television. In 1979 Survival also became the first to sell wildlife films to China. The following year, it launched its first children's show, *Animals in Action* with wildlife artist Keith Shackleton.

In the USA, National Geographic entered the filmmaking business in 1963, though not initially with wildlife films. Hugo van Lawick's *Miss Jane Goodall and*

Her Chimpanzees was its first natural history acquisition, narrated in the USA by Orson Welles. This was the first of many specials networked on CBS. In 1966, ABC countered with *The Undersea World of Jacques Cousteau.*

Back in the UK, Oxford Scientific Films was formed in 1968, specializing at first in macro-, micro-, high-speed and time-lapse photography (see Chapter Seven), and in 1974 Mike Rosenberg launched Partridge Films as a producer of high-profile, blue-chip films such as David Hughes' enchanting *Etosha: The Place of Dry Water*, which aired on the *The World About Us*, and Phil Agland's *Korup: An African Rainforest*, for Channel 4.

Elsewhere in the world, major broadcasters were also moving into wildlife film-making. In 1973, ABC Australia set up its own unit in Melbourne, although it had been producing wildlife films since 1956, and later in the decade, Television New Zealand started its Dunedin-based unit, with its award-winning *Wild South* series becoming a favourite with viewers down under.

Seeing Things in a Different Light

On the BBC, meanwhile, technology was taking wildlife programming in a familiar direction – the outside broadcast – but giving it a different twist. *Night of the Fox* (1976) included the first live television pictures of fox behaviour at night. Specially adapted, remote-controlled cameras spied on a fox's den and infrared lights enabled the audience to see events as they unfolded, even in complete darkness. Yet the animals could behave normally, unaware of their watching audience. Zoologist David MacDonald, from Oxford University, was one of the commentators. The show not only provided entertainment for late-night viewers, but also gathered data of value to science (a dual purpose that wildlife films continue to serve, as we shall see in Chapter Nine).

The following year saw Bruce Parker and the infrared television team applying the same techniques in *Badgerwatch*, and *Reefwatch* soon took them under water. Since then there have been many 'livewatch' programmes, starting with *Birdwatch* (1980) at the Wildfowl Trust at Slimbridge, where Peter Scott, Tony Soper and artist and entertainer Rolf Harris waxed lyrical about wild geese and swans. It was so successful that a more adventurous bird watch was arranged from the RSPB's reserve at Minsmere, where the 'stars' of the show were avocets. Six cameras dotted about the reserve brought no fewer than 25 bird species into viewers' living rooms. Even more elaborate outside broadcasts followed – from the Camargue, Florida, the Netherlands, Bass Rock and the Farne Islands. Paul Appleby, one of the producers on the Farne

Islands and Bass Rock broadcasts, remembers how, true to form, the British weather was totally unreliable:

'We had terrible weather on the Bass Rock. We couldn't see the rock at all. We knew it was out there in the mist somewhere. All the zoom lenses on the cameras had packed in because of the damp. At one point, just before we were going on the air for a 15-minute live programme, we couldn't see the rock, we couldn't see any birds, none of the cameras could zoom and we were having terrible trouble with the communications. We just had to go for it and there was a big team with everybody working together – a lovely feeling. And it's real. The birds were sitting on the rock because they couldn't fly in the mist. It was real life. You would never go out and film this. You'd stay in the hotel and look at the rain, but we were committed to a slot in BBC1's valuable airtime. So the audience saw things that we wouldn't normally see, because it wasn't up to the standard of filming that we normally expect.'

It wasn't always that bad, however:

'One of the best sequences was with Tony Soper on Staple Island, one of the Farnes. He had read that if you present some vegetation to a shag, it would take it and incorporate it into its nest, so we thought we'd try it live, no rehearsals. He put a piece of sea campion next to the nest and the bird immediately picked it up and very delicately weaved it into the nest. Tony was completely bowled over.'

There were also times when the drama unfolding in front of the camera was almost too much for the production crews to bear. Producer Robin Prytherch remembers two occasions when young birds were in serious trouble and it was difficult for the team not to intervene. The first instance was in the Netherlands:

PRYTHERCH, *BIRDWATCH*

'A herring gull came down and tried to lift off one of the birds and kill it. It kept doing this for several minutes, picking up the baby flamingo by the head and dropping it time and time again. It was excruciating to watch it happening right in front of the cameras.'

'We had a tense situation develop with a nest of cormorants we were watching closely. A sub-adult bird had come in and taken over the nest containing two chicks while the parents were away at sea. The sub-adult was trying to evict the chicks, but they clung on for dear life while the older bird was hammering them on the back of the neck and on their wings. In the filming hide, the crew were willing the parents to return and it was a spectacular moment when one of them flew in and hit the sub-adult bird, the two falling to the ground. The relief we all felt that the chicks were safe was extraordinary.'

The second occasion was one of television's classic moments. The outside broadcast team were in the Camargue watching crèches of young flamingos being harassed by gulls:

'There were one or two little ones who couldn't keep up with the main group and got left behind. A herring gull came down and tried to lift off one of the birds and kill it. It kept doing this for several minutes, picking up the baby flamingo by the head and dropping it time and time again. It was excruciating to watch it happening right in front of the cameras. After we recorded the sequence we were looking at it and wondering whether we could let it run in the programme. It was a difficult decision.'

It reminded Robin of a similar occasion on an outside broadcast from a Scottish cliffside, when an older kittiwake chick was pecking mercilessly at its younger sibling:

'The engineering manager had to leave the scanner. He couldn't bear to watch. He said, "You can't possibly show that; it's just too awful." In fact, we did show some of it, but it was so gruesome, we had to edit it. In real life, it went on and on and on – you cannot believe it can go on for so long. You wonder how these birds can cope with it, but in the end they actually win through. Our job is to show this, but maybe show it in an acceptable form. The question is do you show these things as they actually happen or do you edit it?'

Animal Soap Operas

Whether to edit or not is the kind of decision that producers of outside broadcasts must often make. In the 2007 series of *Springwatch* (of which we shall hear more later in this chapter), for example, the first week of transmissions saw no fewer than three dramatic incidents showing baby owls and buzzards eating their siblings in front of the cameras.

The predecessor to *Springwatch* was a series called *Nest Side Story* (1989). The production team was tasked with finding the most bizarre bird-nesting sites in the country and it was Hilary Jeffkins's job to follow up the phone calls and letters.

'We had notices all over the place – post offices, newsagents, women's magazines – saying, "If you see a kinky nest, let us know" and we were bombarded with people phoning up and writing about their birds' nests. I had quite a lot of nice little old ladies telling me about nests they had seen 20 years previously, but one of the letters I remember well was a man who wrote about a nest in an old vacuum cleaner at the end of his garden. He described beautifully what was going on, but he didn't

Left: Presenter and cameraman Simon King and one of the animal soap stars from Big Cat Diary.

Below: The Big Cat Diary *film crew in their camera car are ignored by a pride of lions.*

say what species it was. I phoned him up and asked him what type he thought it was, and he said, "It's a Hoover"'.

British wildlife has always had a place in the BBC's schedules. The long-running series *In the Country,* presented by Angela Rippon, featured guests such as countryman Phil Drabble, artist Gordon Beningfield, rare breeds expert Joe Henson, ornithologist Roger Lovegrove and botanist Richard Mabey. It was produced by Peter Crawford, who went on to give us such exotic extravaganzas as *Global Sunrise,* which took viewers 'live' around the world to see the sunrise on different continents, the kind of undertaking that only the BBC has the wherewithal and ambition to stage.

In 1996, the NHU pioneered the 'animal soap' with its ambitious and very popular *Big Cat Diary*. The ease with which presenters Jonathan Scott, Simon King and more recently Saba Douglas-Hamilton have followed the adventures of the leopards Bella and Half-tail, Honey the cheetah and the Marsh Pride of lions is only possible because of the unusually large production team in the field and the novel way in which the programmes are put together.

The *Big Cat* operation is based in a large tented camp in the Masai Mara National Park and involves over 70 people ranging from camera crews and presenters to cooks and bottle-washers. Each charismatic animal – cheetah, leopard and lion – has a dedicated presenter, director-DV camera operator, wildlife camera-person, and at least two spotters. The leopard crew has two extra spotters as leopards are so elusive. One sound recordist gathers natural sounds and two editors supported by two assistant editors cut the rushes the moment the crews return to camp. The entire operation is overseen by a series producer. In the early days, one of the team would hotfoot the transmission tape back to the UK for transmission that week, but more recently the latter stages of post-production (see Chapter Four) have been completed at a (slightly) more leisurely pace in Bristol

The series has been running for ten years, although in 2004 it transformed into *Big Cat Week* and was transmitted with considerable success early on five consecutive evenings on BBC1. Viewers even book safari holidays to Kenya just to see their favourite animal soap stars. Spin-off series have included *Elephant Diaries*, in which Michaela Strachan and Jonathan Scott followed the fortunes of a group of orphaned elephants and charted their journey back to the wild. In *Orang-Utan Diary*, Michaela and Steve Leonard met orphaned and rescued animals in Borneo. Saba and Jonathan were joined by Canadian filmmaker Jeff Turner to track polar, grizzly and black bears in *Big Bear Week*. All have been hugely successful in an early evening slot stripped across a week.

Putting Words in Their Mouths

The NHU is also one of the few wildlife filmmaking companies to make programmes for all ages. Since 1958, it has produced a regular programme for children, starting with the monthly *Out of Doors*, presented by Bruce Campbell. Even in those days, the NHU's programmes aimed at being 'inclusive' rather than 'exclusive', and in this series the audience was introduced to a new face – Leslie Jackman, a schoolteacher from Devon who ran a small summer aquarium in Paignton. Jackman was given a regular slot, first commenting on the various fish brought into the harbour by a local fishing boat and then, from January 1959, hosting a monthly 'Club Room' that encouraged children to go out into the countryside and make bark rubbings, plaster casts of animal footprints and such like. The young viewers were invited to send their models and pictures to the studio and each one of them received a special club badge and was deemed a member of the *Out of Doors* club. By the end of 1960, there were more than 11,000 club members; in 1961, the number doubled.

In 1962, NHU producer Winwood Reade was tasked with coming up with a new children's series with a new title and a new presenter. The magic of animals was acceptable as a concept, so *Animal Magic* became the title, but who should present it? Winwood Reade was looking for a particular type of presenter, in his words: 'An entertainer who already has star quality who is prepared to share the limelight with animals.' Ace storyteller Johnny Morris was already known on radio and as the 'Hot

Johnny Morris and friend at Bristol Zoo at the time of Animal Magic.

Chestnut Man' in the children's show *Crackerjack*; he had also written and read the narration for Bertil Danielsson's prize-winning Swedish film *Tufty* (1957), about tufted ducks, and had similarly brought his own brand of mischief and humour to *The Unknown Forest* (1959), including footage by Eric Ashby showing badgers and foxes coming out in the daytime rather than at night. There was, however, something of a dilemma for a department that had prided itself on being scientifically sound.

In *Animal Magic*, Morris took on the persona of a keeper at nearby Bristol Zoo, and not only voiced the thoughts in his own head but also what he felt was in the heads of the animals he visited, together with the appropriate voices. The result was very entertaining and children loved it, but was it acceptable in a factual programme? Desmond Hawkins thought so:

'Johnny Morris brought a new element into wildlife programmes,' he recalled, 'in some ways a controversial element because Johnny had this extraordinary knack of somehow narrowing the gap between human beings and animals. He moved into their world and they moved into ours; and this of course raised the bogey of anthropomorphism – you are reading into animals things that belong to human beings but are untrue of them.

'Now, in a fictional cartoon, such as *Bambi,* you are really falsifying the behaviour of the deer. I mean, you are suggesting that the father deer has a paternal interest in the young deer, which of course in nature does not happen at all. Johnny did not tell biological lies. He somehow mediated between the viewer and the animal.'

Morris had acquired his knack from being brought up with a talking parrot – an African grey, a species noted not only for its ability to talk but also for its intelligence. 'It talked to me,' Morris once recalled, 'and I talked to it. It could think, and of course it talked, and I applied this to other animals. Well, they don't talk like the parrot did, but I put words in their mouths for them.'

Animal Magic launched on 13 April 1962 and ran for 22 years with over 400 editions. Regular animal visitors such as Dottie the lemur usually joined Morris in the studio, and there were human visitors, too, including Tony Soper, Keith Shackleton, David Taylor, Gerald Durrell and a young Terry Nutkins. Terry had worked with Gavin Maxwell and his otters in Scotland and was adept at handling animals (although he lost two fingers to an angry otter called Edal while with Maxwell). *Animal Magic* was live from the Bristol studios, and producer Peter Crawford remembers how it was often when the show was 'on air' that things went wrong:

Johnny Morris and Terry Nutkins in the Animal Magic *studio.*

'I remember an orang-utan, which came from Bristol Zoo, which was wheeled into the studio whenever we had a programme that was a little light and needed a filler towards the end. In fact, there were two orang-utans, and I christened them Gary and Baldy. They would come into the studio, and Baldy was a little fed up about the way we pulled his leg about his hair, and right on the end credits, when Johnny picked him up, he peed in his pocket.

It was on the side that had the radio mic, so we had a very soggy end to the programme. After that, Gary was asked back, but Baldy never returned.'

Running alongside *Animal Magic* for several years was *Wildtrack*, which launched in 1978 with Tony Soper and Sue Ingle looking at Britain's wildlife from the perspective of young viewers. In later programmes, Terry Nutkins and Michael Jordan joined as co-presenters.

Chris Packham, Terry Nutkins and Michaela Strachan in The Really Wild Show *studio.*

In 1984, the anthropomorphic approach adopted by Johnny Morris fell out of favour and, to ensure some continuity, Terry Nutkins and two new presenters, Nick Davies and Chris Packham, were invited to front a brand-new children's series, *The Really Wild Show*. It started in January 1986 and ran for 20 years, picking up three BAFTA awards during that time and evolving from a circus-style studio-based show with an audience of children to a mainly film-based programme. Producer Hilary Jeffkins remembers the early days:

'It was the most challenging combination. You had something like 100 to 120 children, and animals coming in all the time. The children had seen the programme on television and, of course, it was 30 minutes of wham, bang, action and fun, but the reality is that it took two days to make. While the show was recorded, the audience had to wait for the animals to be in the right position and the presenters to say the right words at the right time. The children couldn't be sticking their fingers in their ears or noses, pulling faces or waving at themselves in the monitors. It was good fun, but there was always one child you would really like to have ushered out of the studio. There was one occasion, for instance, that we were doing a piece about geckos and the presenter was asking the question, "How do you think geckos stick onto the glass?" And there was one little chap who had obviously read about it and he yelled, "Ah well, it has flaps of skin on its feet and they form a vacuum and stick on the glass." They were meant to say, "I don't know," so we had to say to the floor manager, "Could you move that child to the back?".

Like *Animal Magic*, *The Really Wild Show* had its amusing moments, such as the time a baby elephant demolished a set in the studio and a chimpanzee would not stop fussing until it had been introduced to and then gently touched a baby monkey, but perhaps the funniest was the jackdaw that was brought in to take part in an animal version of *Mastermind*. It was too clever by half, and eventually flew up into the studio lighting gantry and would not come down. Its trainer said, 'Not to worry, it'll be safe up there, I'll collect it in the morning,' and everyone went home. Unknown to the production team, however, a political discussion was taking place in the same studio the following day. Before they could recover the jackdaw, the programme was under way. You can imagine the surprise on the guests' faces when halfway through the live transmission a jackdaw swooped down from the studio ceiling. One viewer wrote in to say the programme was dull, except for the bit where the big black bird flew by!

The Really Wild Show reinvented itself several times, with various presenters coming and going, including Michaela Strachan, Howie Watkins, Nick Baker, Janice Acquah, Eils Hewitt and Steve Backshall. Often the show would focus on a particular country or issue, with one moving episode on the trade in bear gall bladders gaining several international awards.

Building Epics

In mainstream wildlife filmmaking, the NHU has been fortunate in having two long-running strands. In 1977, *Wildlife on One* appeared on BBC1 with an amusing film about albatrosses on Midway Island in the South Pacific called *The Bird that Beat the US Navy*. It was the first of a series of half-hour films, narrated by David Attenborough, which ran very successfully until it was axed in 2005, curiously at a time when it was attracting its largest audiences

David Attenborough with mountain gorillas while filming for Life on Earth.

in the peak-time schedules. And by 1993, *The World About Us* had run its course on BBC2 and was replaced by *Natural World*. The first film in the new strand was a National Geographic special, *Save the Panda,* which focused on the plight of giant pandas in the wake of the widespread flowering and dying back of bamboo. Today, *Natural World* is one of the last bastions on British television of the single 50-minute wildlife documentary.

Alongside these established series there have, of course, been the epics, the first of which was *Life on Earth* in 1979. Following a period as Director of Programmes, overseeing both BBC channels, David Attenborough felt that the call of the wild was too great for him to remain behind a desk. After a sojourn in Southeast Asia with *Eastward with Attenborough* (1973) and then an exposition on *Tribal Art* (1975), he joined with the Natural History Unit, working on the proposed new series with executive producer Christopher Parsons.

LIFE ON EARTH

It was one of the first BBC programmes to enter into an international co-production agreement. It was also the first time that a presenter started a piece to camera in one country and finished it in another.

Chris and his boss Nicholas Crocker had quite a fight on their hands. At that time, London was not convinced that the people in Bristol had the wherewithal to deliver such a mammoth series … but they did, and 20 million people in Britain and an estimated 500 million worldwide watched the 13 enthralling episodes. *Life on Earth* traced the evolution of life, and five years later *The Living Planet* (1984) featured the Earth's major biomes, with episodes featuring, for example, 'Furnaces of the Earth' and 'The Frozen World'. In 1990, the life trilogy was completed with the *Trials of Life*, an exposition of animal behaviour. It put the NHU on the world map as a producer of quality wildlife films, and it has remained there ever since.

Life on Earth, however, was not only noted for its pictures and presenter. It was one of the first BBC programmes to enter into an international co-production agreement. It was also the first time that a presenter started a piece to camera in one country and finished it in another. It was a global view, and not only a turning point for the NHU, but also a significant moment for its presenter.

'The production team got together,' recalls Attenborough, 'and they said, "Somebody's got to tell Attenborough that he mustn't really go on wearing shorts. It was all right when he was a boy scout, hopping around in his twenties, but he's older than that now. We don't think shorts become him! We think," they said, "he should wear a safari suit." As you well know, presenters are mere putty in the hands of their production team, so I put up no opposition, I was simply told what I had to do and I was sent off to buy myself a safari suit ... actually four safari suits, the theory being that I always had the right attire for continuity purposes. No matter where I was, I had to have a crisp, neatly ironed safari suit. I was wearing one of these natty little numbers when we were doing a sequence about a forest fire. We went to one of these fires in the southern United States and the place was absolutely smoking. There were logs spouting jets of smoke, and they said, "That's fine, stand in the middle there and do a piece to camera." So I went in amongst the burning embers and smoke, and it was frightfully hot, and I looked at the camera and started my piece, and I thought this is really hot, so I was relieved to come to the end of the rather long monologue. Then the cameraman and director burst out laughing. "What's so funny?" I asked and they said, "We didn't want to interrupt you as it was going so well, but look down." I looked down to see that my trousers were on fire!'

Nigel Marven and Nicolai Drozdov during the making of Realms of the Russian Bear.

Hard on the heels of the success of *Life on Earth*, in 1982 the 'mini-series' entered the BBC television vocabulary: producer Mike Andrews made a special three-part series on the South American Andes for *The World About Us*. This was *Flight of the Condor*, remembered today as much for its evocative title music as for the stunning images captured by such talented cameramen as Hugh Miles and Roger Jackman. It gave rise to many more, including Mike Salisbury's *Kingdom of the Ice Bear* (1985), shot by Hugh Miles and Martin Saunders.

Uncharted Territories

Throughout its history, the NHU has been quick to take advantage of any new travel opportunities and has often been among the first to gain access to countries previously closed to journalists. In October 1961, for example, at the height of the Cold War, the series *World Zoos* piggybacked a BBC outside broadcast from the May Day

The Planet Earth *film crew had to get special permission to film over the Himalayas where cranes migrate 6000 metres (20,000 feet) over the mountains.*

parade in Moscow and visited Moscow Zoo. The usual presenter, James Fisher, was unavailable, so David Attenborough was invited to stand in. It was the first time he had worked for the NHU and possibly the first time he had romped with a baby bear. Some years later, when relations between East and West were warming and the Berlin Wall was falling down, Russian naturalist and television presenter Nicolai Drozdov – the 'David Attenborough' of the former Soviet Union – presented *Realms of the Russian Bear* for the BBC. The NHU's film crews were allowed previously unheard-of access to almost all parts of the country. Over the course of six weeks viewers were taken to see the lunar-like, active volcanic region of Kamchatka, the seals of Lake Baikal – the planet's oldest and deepest lake – and an extraordinary sequence filmed by Martin Saunders showing polar bears attacking huge numbers of walrus on Wrangel Island in the Russian Arctic.

In 1988 Jean-Paul Davidson and cameraman Richard Ganniclift were given special permission to enter Bhutan and film *Kingdom of the Thunder Dragon* for *Natural World*. Colourful dancing festivals attended by local people were juxtaposed with a natural ballet of black-necked cranes. Currently, a groundbreaking collaboration with Chinese television has given film crews unprecedented access to produce a series of films with the working title *Wild China*.

In Nepal and Pakistan it took almost a year's negotiating with the authorities to obtain permission to film golden eagles attacking cranes migrating at 6,000 metres (20,000 feet) over the Himalayas for the landmark high-definition series *Planet Earth*. It took two years to obtain permission to film in the Lechuguilla Caves in New Mexico, *Planet Earth's* crew being the last to be allowed in there, and two years to be permitted to film on the Tibetan plateau. *Planet Earth* was the culmination of five years' work at 204 locations worldwide with a 70-strong production team and camera crew, possibly the ultimate wildlife television series.

Today, the genre has come full circle. The live outside broadcast is still alive and well. *Springwatch*, from a farm in Devon and a remote location in the Scottish islands, is presented by Bill Oddie, Kate Humble and Simon King. With its website and other interactive media it emphasizes 'empowerment' – what the audience can do to experience the natural world themselves. The NHU has also returned to the movies with a sumptuous feature simply titled *Earth*, a spin-off from *Planet Earth*. And a new variation on nature's 'little comedians' has found its way into the cinema too – not Cherry Kearton's penguins (though emperor penguins had an outing in the French Academy Award®-winning movie *March of the Penguins* in 2005) – but meerkats, with not one but two rival productions hitting our cinema screens in 2007. It is a far cry technologically from Oliver Pike's *In Birdland*, yet the same integrity and pioneering spirit prevails.

SPRINGWATCH

Confirmation that British television audiences like watching their own wildlife came with the phenomenal success of the BBC's seasonal *Springwatch* and *Autumnwatch*. Presented 'live' by Bill Oddie, Kate Humble and Simon King, the programmes are stripped across the schedules each weekday evening for three weeks, with the addition of night-time transmissions – *Springwatch Nightshift* – in the 2007 season. The operation is a mammoth outside broadcast event staged at a 163-hectare (403-acre) organic farm in Devon, with satellite feeds from Scottish islands such as Islay and Bass Rock, and contributions from wildlife sites around the country, including the Lost Gardens of Heligan in Cornwall. At the farm, more than 50 cameras monitor owls, buzzards, kingfishers, badgers, otters and other wildlife, and are linked by nearly 60 kilometres (40 miles) of fibre-optic, camera and power cables to 220 television monitors in control rooms, editing suites and viewing rooms in a temporary production 'village'. A further 21 cameras located in different parts of the UK are accessed by satellite. The crew numbers close to a hundred people, including producers, directors, researchers, runners, production co-ordinators, production managers, camera operators, sound recordists, and television and telecommunications engineers. Working in shifts around the clock, observers watch every move the animals make, noting the highlights for the three and a half hours of daily *Springwatch* broadcasts which, in addition to the regular evening slot, include contributions to BBC News 24 and to various national and regional television and radio programmes, as well as a special children's version, *CBeebies Springwatch*. Pre-recorded inserts include short films about people who are passionate about wildlife, both in urban and rural settings, videos from viewers, and pre-recorded 'diaries', such as Fox Diary, which was filmed by wildlife cameraman Gordon Buchanan and featured urban foxes in Glasgow. The *Springwatch* website encourages people to get out and about to see wildlife for themselves, with Breathing Places and family fun days out in collaboration with BBC local radio, and partnerships with conservation organizations such as the RSPB, Bat Conservation Trust and Woodland Trust. Viewers have been contributing to nationwide surveys of plants and animals, such as bumblebees, ladybirds, butterflies, swifts and hawthorn, and every household has been urged to 'do one thing' to help their local wildlife. All in all, *Springwatch* has become more than a television programme; it is almost a way of life.

Above: Bill Oddie on Springwatch.

[CHAPTER FOUR]

Anatomy of a Wildlife Team

In some respects, wildlife filmmaking is different from any other form. For one thing, it takes a lot longer. A conventional documentary might be researched in six to eight weeks, shot in three to eight, followed by an editing period of six weeks or less, so the whole production can be turned around and broadcast well within a year – and as often as not in less than six months. A wildlife film, on the other hand, often follows an animal's life cycle or a season-by-season description of a place, so right there is at least a year's commitment. In fact, it might be two years because the filmmaker will want to film specific things and there's no guarantee of success first time round. ☞

Above: David Attenborough sitting beside giant tortoises in Aldabra, Indian Ocean.

Dedication's What You Need

For a major series, where there is a complex matrix of many wildlife behaviour stories in several different countries, filming can easily take two or three years. The starting point, whether a film is to be made within the NHU or by an independent producer, is nothing more complicated than an idea. It may be a mere twinkle in the eye, some vague notion, a half-heard rumour of some surprising behaviour or a place where hundreds or even thousands of individuals of a particular species gather. It might start with a place or an animal, with a person or simply a whim, but whatever the subject, the idea must be practical.

Underwater cameraman Doug Allan films a humpback whale mother and calf off the South Pacific island of Tonga for Planet Earth.

Every wildlife filmmaker in the world would love to capture the gargantuan battle between a sperm whale and a giant squid in the inky depths of the sea, and many have considered doing so, but how do you film it? Squid shun light and sperm whales are sensitive to sound, and anyway how do you get cameras into the deep, way beyond the depths to which human divers can go? Can you afford deep-sea submersibles and the mother ship that comes with them? Even if you get down there, how do you find your stars in the featureless abyss and, having found them once, how do you track them down again? With so few sightings and even fewer pictures of a giant squid in its natural environment, it is surprising that anybody would even try, but several have, losing many millions of dollars in the attempt. So an idea for a

wildlife film cannot be completely 'pie in the sky'.

At one time, producers could have put a pin into a map virtually anywhere in the world and guarantee finding something that had not been filmed before. Today, however, with restricted budgets and the pressure to deliver natural spectacle and wildlife action, ideas have to be well researched and the subjects have to be accessible and able to be filmed in the shortest possible time. Even with a landmark series, these restraints apply to the individual programmes or sequences.

Research is the key to an effective and efficient wildlife film. After the initial idea has been accepted by the commissioner (the BBC has several such people, so ideas coming from inside the NHU are submitted to the commissioner for natural history, those from producers on the outside go to the person charged with commissioning from 'independents') the story is fleshed out. This involves a huge amount of legwork – searching books and scientific papers, surfing the Internet and talking to scientists. In fact, without the help of scientists, especially those in the field, very few of today's wildlife films would be made at all.

Producer Huw Cordey in the rainforest canopy in Costa Rica for the 'Jungle' episode of Planet Earth.

Research workers sometimes have a greater knowledge of wildlife activities in an area than the people who actual live and work there. Cameraman Martyn Colbeck discovered this when working in the Masai Mara in Kenya. He was filming a topi lek, the place where the males of this antelope species advertise their prowess by prancing about. Many are exhausted by late morning and, in the heat of the mid-day sun, they lie down and rest.
At this point, hyenas appear, hunting not in packs but individually, and taking the topis before they have time to get up. Martyn wanted to film this behaviour, but even people working in the Mara, who are generally very knowledgeable about the wildlife living there, were unaware that hyenas behaved in this way. However, a scientist who was making a detailed study of topis was able to guide Martyn and his team to be in the right place at the right time.

Martyn's experience illustrates just how crucial scientists working in the field are to successful filming. A casual walk in the rainforest, for example, is unlikely to reveal anything, so the first step for the filmmaker is to find somebody who is familiar with the area and knows the behaviour of the species to be filmed. These are the only people able to reveal its secrets.

A casual walk in the rainforest, for example, is unlikely to reveal anything, so the first step for the film-maker is to find somebody who is familiar with the area and knows the behaviour of the species to be filmed. These are the only people able to reveal its secrets.

Equally important is the trust between scientists and filmmakers. Over the years, the NHU and many of the other established production companies have built a reputation for taking natural history seriously; for neither sensationalizing it nor being sloppy with the science. After all, the filmmaker is meeting people who have dedicated themselves to a particular group of animals, are fascinated by them and care for them.

For example, when one of the production team of *The Trials of Life* was talking to Christophe Boesch, director of primatology at the German-based Max Planck Institute, Christophe let slip that chimpanzees were not the cuddly charmers we had all come to know and love, but violent hunters with a taste for monkey meat – he had seen them hunting colobus monkeys. This information led to an extremely dramatic and, for most people, surprising sequence in the episode on 'Hunting and Escaping'. Without Christophe's field observations and the trust he had that his work would not be misrepresented, the team would have had no story to tell.

Money Makes the World Go Round

Once the story is in place, the film has to be costed. It is all well and good putting forward an incredible story with the expectation of spectacular images, but is it affordable? Virtually every stage of the production has a price, for nothing these days is free. There was a time when film crews could visit exotic locations for nothing, but today national park authorities and private landowners alike demand a fee. Budgets have had to rise, with 'blue-chip' wildlife films costing almost as much as costume dramas ... and if you go to sea, multiply everything by three.

As a consequence of its co-production partnerships, the BBC's NHU is one of the few production units in the world able to mount themed landmark series, in which each episode contributes to an overall story. This approach differs from 'strands', such as BBC1's *Wildlife on One*, BBC2's *Natural World* or PBS's *Nature*, in which each episode is self-contained and not necessarily linked to the programme broadcast the previous or next week. Landmark series are expensive to make, and for these the BBC must seeks partners, such as Discovery Channel, Animal Planet, National Geographic and WNET New York *Nature*, part of the public service network in the USA. Across the world, ORF-Austria, SDF-Germany, SVT-Sweden, NDR-Norway and ABC Australia have been close associates of the BBC at one time or another. These are all stations that champion wildlife films; indeed several have successful natural history units of their own. Without these partnerships large and expensive wildlife films would be impossible to make.

With the finances in place, the final preparatory stage is to persuade the commissioners that the film is viable. Wherever and with whom, the commissioning process is often long and drawn out, and it has always been that way. Such is the pressure on television companies to succeed – especially on commercial television channels, where advertising revenue is vital to their very survival – that channel controllers and commissioners have to get it right first time round; as a result, risk-taking is minimal. Fortunately for UK television audiences, there has always been an atmosphere in the BBC in which innovation is encouraged, even when times are tough, so the NHU is often at the forefront of new programme development, rather than following a trend.

With the programme commissioned and the finances in place, the project is ready to start. Staff are appointed – series producers to look after several programmes in a series, producers for individual programmes, assistant producers to take charge of programme segments, and researchers to track down just about everything that's needed to make the whole thing work. Scientists in the field feed back information on the best locations and times of year. Production co-ordinators plan

Filming a king cobra for The Serpent's Embrace, *an edition of the* Natural World *in 1990.*

how to move people and equipment from home base to filming locations in the most efficient yet least expensive way. Production managers keep the whole thing on track and on schedule and watch the bottom line. It is a logistical nightmare, yet somehow it all works.

Routes and Recces

With the team in place, everything steps up a gear. Sometimes producers need to take a look for themselves before committing to a major filming operation. This is the recce (reconnaissance). An advance party heads out into the great unknown, checking on places and things, establishing whether it is practical to film something that started as a theoretical possibility, whether local transport is where it should be and runs when the timetable says it does, whether the natural spectacle really does look spectacular, whether the sun is on one side of a valley or the other at the intended time of filming, whether the guide really does speak English and where a hot shower and edible food are to be found. If things are too vague or too chancy a producer might even now pull the plug and abandon the shoot altogether. If it all falls into place, however, the entire production machine starts to move.

Sometimes a recce is not practical. Many natural events are unpredictable, so there are occasions when the film crew need to be able to move quickly. During the filming of *The Living Planet*, for example, the production team was on standby for a volcanic eruption in Iceland and David Attenborough waited patiently for word:

'I'm a trustee of the British Museum and I was sitting in a trustees' meeting, which is a very dignified affair, when a museum official came in and handed me a note on a silver salver. I read the note and spoke to the chairman, who was a noble lord at the time. I said, "My Lord, I hope you'll excuse me, I have to leave urgently – there's a volcano exploding."

'So I left, having made quite an exit. I went by taxi to my home, where I picked up my bag and we drove straight to Heathrow and just made it for the plane to

Cameraman Hugh Maynard and sound recordists 'Red' Denner filming in the snow for Living Planet.

Iceland. We landed in the middle of the night in a blizzard, and there was a small charter plane waiting to fly us to the northern side of the island. In the early hours of the morning we finally arrived to the most marvellous sight – a plume of scarlet lava shooting up a hundred, two hundred feet into the air. We filmed this for a while, getting a variety of shots. By the time we had finished, it was dawn and having been filming all night we were very tired. As we arrived at a little guest house, an enormous plane landed and out came 20 or 30 people, a German film crew, I recall. One of them came over to me and said, "We are hearing there's an eruption, where is this eruption, please?" I said, "Well, you just go down there, carry on along the glacier, etc., etc." So they all shot off and we resuscitated ourselves with fried eggs and bacon. Two hours later, they all came back again and the leader said, "It was finished!" I couldn't restrain a little laugh.'

Most film excursions start with the same headache. How do you carry all the blessed equipment through British customs, on to aeroplanes, through foreign customs and onward to the location?

On this occasion, David Attenborough's crew had been on standby for a well-rehearsed getaway. Most have to contend with the vagaries of international travel. Task one is getting to the airport. Easy, you might say, but producer Tim Martin, working on the three-part series *Violent Planet* in 1999, might not agree. He had the onerous task of carrying a model of a giant anaconda to South America. It really was 'giant', so he had booked a large estate car to take it to the airport. Things began to go wrong when he came down in the morning to find the car's wheels had been stolen. The rest of the journey was like a rerun of the classic John Cleese film *Clockwise*, when everything that could possibly go wrong, did.

Travelling by car in the UK is not normally too hazardous, but when a crew reaches its destination car travel can mean something else altogether. Peter Jones and his film crew were on location in India for a costume drama about the great tiger-hunter-turned-conservationist Jim Corbett:

'You are either going up or down really inaccessible roads, tracks and slopes, hairpin bends, and 1000-foot drops on each side of the road. At one point the first car carrying the cameraman and the director lost its brakes, but they were able to steer it into the side of the road and come to a halt. Minutes later, the next vehicle lost its steering, but at least they had their brakes and were able to pull in.'

Most film excursions, however, start with the same headache. How do you carry all the blessed equipment through British customs, on to aeroplanes, through foreign customs and onward to the location? Imagine turning up at Heathrow with 30 pieces of luggage – film equipment, medical supplies, cans of film and all the paraphernalia essential to a wildlife filming expedition – and it all has to be checked in. For *Big Cat Diary* and *Big Cat Week*, it is not only the camera gear that has to be shipped out, but also the entire office, editing suites and all. Getting all this through the airport authorities in the UK is one thing, but seeing it through customs at the other end is another. It can take the best part of a day or more.

And That's the Easy Bit

Having managed that and then travelled on to some remote part of the country, another problem is money, especially when buying supplies. As often as not, cash in the form of US dollars, or traveller's cheques in dollars or sterling, are preferred, but when producer Karen Bass went to a remote town in the Urals, to film for *The First Eden* in1987, she was in for a shock:

'I had some roubles, but the local traders wanted *everything* paid in roubles, so I thought, "OK, I'll change some money". The first problem was there wasn't a bank, so I spent some time ringing around to find the nearest one ... they agreed to change some money for me, but that was a three-hour drive through a frozen wasteland. I eventually got there, but when I presented them with traveller's cheques, they looked at me and said, "What's this?" It was a bank, but they'd never seen a traveller's cheque before. So I said, "What about some dollars cash?" They looked at them, but they weren't sure. They'd seen pictures of dollars, but had never handled the real thing – they had to ring their superiors to see if the transaction was OK. I thought, "If it's going to be this difficult, I'd better change quite a lot." So I produced $4,000, which took them aback, and then used my pocket calculator to do the calculation, but to my horror they brought out a wooden abacus upon which they worked out the exchange ... it took two and a half hours!'

With all the preparation and logistical problems involved in getting to the location, you could be forgiven for thinking the actual filming (see Chapter Six) was the easy bit. There are a few tricks of the trade that help. Animals habituated to people are less difficult to film, as they accept the presence of camera crews. In parts of East Africa, for example, many of the large carnivores are so used to tourist vehicles that they take no notice of them, and to the wildlife a camera car is just like all the other trucks and buses. It becomes part of the landscape. Cheetahs in the Masai Mara even use them as lookouts, totally ignoring the people inside. It makes it easier to achieve an exciting week of programmes in a series like *Big Cat Week*, but even this can have its drawbacks. Jonathan Scott was in the camera car when a cheetah urinated over him, quite oblivious to his being there.

In popular holiday destinations such as the Mara, though, tourist buses can be a problem, not only because there are so many of them, but also because the drivers tend to look for the filmmakers. They know that a camera car is where the action is. However, most tourist vehicles follow a set routine and a crafty cameraman can work around it. Producer Mike Salisbury and his cameraman did just that on the last day of filming cheetahs in Kenya. They still had to get a good chase sequence and saw an opportunity when the tourists had gone back to camp for lunch:

'It was a grey day. We were watching this one cheetah and were almost falling asleep when I looked up and saw that she was about to move. We looked around and, yes, there was a Thomson's gazelle that she was probably going to go for. The cameraman said, "Oh, but the light is terrible." I said, "If she goes for it we must film it," but he said, "It's really going to look awful." At that moment a gap in the clouds came and a shaft of sunlight lit the scene. I said, "She'd better be quick, because those tourist vehicles will be back soon." Suddenly, she set off and the cameraman was getting some fantastic shots, but then he said, "I'm running out of camera angle" and then "Doesn't matter, she's changed direction in front of the camera." He was able to get a marvellous long shot and we cheered. At that moment, the sun went in and all the tourists arrived. It was perfect timing – a moment of luck that made it all worthwhile.'

In parts of East Africa many of the large carnivores are so used to tourist vehicles that they take no notice of them, and to the wildlife a camera car is just like all the other trucks and buses.

Imagine, though, the disappointment of a camera crew returning from an especially difficult expedition to New Guinea where they had filmed the courtship behaviour of McGregor's bird of paradise for *The Life of Birds*. At the airport the film was passed through a powerful new X-ray machine designed to detect explosives – it was completely ruined. Tribal unrest prevented the crew from returning to try again. All that effort had been wasted.

With the film safely 'in the can' and through airport security, the crew return to base with many kilometres of film or video, far more than will end up in the final programme, so it must be edited. All the best shots and supporting footage – the wide shots, medium shots, close-ups and cutaways – are collected together and transformed into sequences, each delivering its part of the overall story. These sequences are gathered into a 'rough assembly', which is honed to a 'rough cut' and finally to a 'fine cut', which culminates in 'picture lock', the point after which the pictures are not edited or rearranged again.

The Right Balance

It is in the editing suite that the sort of decisions mentioned in Chapter Three – about what to show or not to show – are made. The old adage 'nature is red in tooth and claw' is more than evident in a hunting sequence involving large carnivores such as lions or hyenas, but whether or not to include the entire event as it happens, blood and all, needs to be considered with caution, especially on television.

The filmmaker, in effect, is invited into somebody's home, so there is 'etiquette' to be observed – it is all too easy to cause offence. Some people, perhaps, sentimentalize the natural world and are blind to the fact that 'violence' is so widespread. Many of those who write to broadcasters complaining of the cruelty shown by, say, lions killing a wildebeest or a crocodile tearing a zebra apart would be amazed or even appalled by what is left 'on the cutting room floor'. The filmmaker treads a narrow line between not sensationalizing violence and not portraying the natural world as some Garden of Eden in which animals just lie down and die.

In most cases, the pictures going through the offline editing process are low-quality copies of the real thing (although with modern computer

Sync crew using a jib arm to film David Attenborough for Life in the Freezer, *South Georgia.*

technology this is gradually changing), so a matching version of high-quality pictures has to be made during a process called the 'conform'. This is followed by the 'grade', during which the colour of the pictures is tweaked, brightening up shots that are underexposed or toning down those that have gone over the top, to give the film an even and clean overall look. It also means that the final script can be written and the sound prepared.

While some sound is recorded on location at the time of filming, especially 'sync sound' with a presenter delivering pieces to camera, much of it is added later in 'post-production'. The key player here is the 'tracklayer' or 'dubbing editor', who puts down several tracks of sound to match events in the picture – for a complex soundtrack, there may be 20 or more. At least one track will contain atmospheres, the ambient sounds of a specific location such as 'daytime in a tropical rainforest in Papua New Guinea', 'nighttime in a Surrey woodland', falling rain or the roar of a waterfall. Further tracks contain calls and songs, such as those of a cuckoo, curlew or chaffinch, or a wolf's howl or the scream of a fox. Many of these will come from the sound library, which stores recordings of wildlife sounds and atmospheres for precisely this purpose.

For a complex soundtrack there may be 20 tracks or more. At least one track will contain atmospheres, the ambient sounds of a specific location such as 'daytime in a tropical rainforest in Papua New Guinea', 'nighttime in a Surrey woodland', falling rain or the roar of a waterfall.

There are some sounds, particularly everyday ones, which are difficult to record on location or get from the library, as they tend to be masked by some other part of the action. These might include the wingbeats of a bird taking off, the splashes of animals entering water, or an animal's footsteps. Such sounds are put on the soundtrack using an array of props, in a process known as 'footsteps' or 'Foleys' that is the responsibility of a specialist film technician known as a 'Foley artist'. The name comes from a pioneering exponent of the technique, one Jack Donovan Foley, who worked at Universal Studios in Hollywood at the beginning of the twentieth century and was one of the first to see a need for adding sounds such as footsteps or the rustling of clothes, in synchrony with events on the screen, for the early 'talkies'.

The odd thing about Foleys is that, as often as not, the real sound is not as effective as a dubbing-theatre substitute. Flapping a pair of leather gloves is fine for the wingbeats of a small bird, while the opening and closing of a half-open umbrella is good for a larger one. The noise of a polar bear's footsteps in snow is created by squeezing corn starch or custard powder inside pantyhose. It may look odd, but it sounds perfect.

BBC dubbing mixer Martyn Harries recalls a time, however, when his producer insisted on the real thing. He had a film sequence showing a fox that had raided a hen house and was noisily feasting on its spoils, so Martyn duly went to the local supermarket and bought a chicken. Unfortunately, the dubbing assistant creating the sound effects was vegetarian, but he pluckily ripped the chicken apart, suppressing the constant desire to throw up, and the sounds were duly recorded. When it was played back, it sounded nothing like a chicken being eaten by a fox, so the assistant resorted to what they had always used – eating an orange!

With such a plethora of tracks, it would be impossible for the dubbing mixer to control them all when mixing the final soundtrack, so the tracks are now 'premixed' to reduce their number. This also produces a rough version of the soundtrack that can be used in the next stage – to give the narrator a 'feel' for the film when he records the commentary.

No-Nonsense Narration

The commentary script is written to the picture, the words matching very precisely events on the screen and sentences written exactly to length for each sequence. Good commentaries guide the viewer, providing just enough information to explain the relevance of the action, without describing what viewers can see for themselves. Words are used sparingly. Adjectives and adverbs are kept to a minimum. There is no room for 'purple prose'.

The audience must also believe what it is being told, so the narrator's voice must match the style of the film. Well-known actors or other celebrities are often asked to narrate wildlife films, but only a few have learned not to intrude – the same actors, incidentally, whose voices are most often heard on television and radio commercials. Narrating a wildlife film, any other form of documentary or even a commercial is not the same as delivering a Shakespeare soliloquy.

Once the right voice is selected, the commentary is recorded in the dubbing theatre. The narrator sits in a small recording booth, in front of a large screen or a television monitor. The rough soundtrack, and the music if it is available, might play into the narrator's headphones and the film comes up on the screen with a time code clearly visible at the top or bottom. Each sentence or paragraph starts at a particular time, so the narrator not only watches for what is going on in the picture but must also be aware of the time to start each cue.

One would not expect such a safe, urban setting as a BBC dubbing theatre to warrant the label 'hazardous', but when the actor Hywel Bennett came to Bristol to narrate *Kingdom of the Ice Bear* in 1985 he discovered it to be full of dangers for the unwary. As he was settling in, he took off his brand-new suede jacket and placed it for safe keeping on the glass-topped table behind the curtain in the commentary booth. The session complete, he and the producer were leaving the theatre when he realized he had forgotten his jacket.

'I'll get it for you,' said an obliging dubbing assistant. 'Where did you leave it?'

'On the glass table,' Bennett replied.

'But we don't have a glass table,' said the assistant.

As they went back into the booth, they realized his mistake. He had placed his jacket not on a glass-topped table, but on the mirror-like surface of the tank of water used for sound effects!

The most controversial element in a wildlife film is, and probably always will be, the music. Some viewers like music; others hate it. When a film has been aired, most letters (emails these days) from 'disgusted of Surbiton' are inevitably about music, either its type or its loudness. (Believe it or not, there are more complaints about music than there are about 'violence' or 'cruelty'.) The wildlife filmmaker would argue, though, that music is an integral part of the programme, helping to create mood and atmosphere, just as in any other film. But music is brought sharply into focus when it has been badly composed or is used inappropriately. For it to do its job properly, as with the narrator's voice we should not notice it is there at all.

With the commentary and music recorded, the programme is ready for what is termed the 'final mix'. Surprisingly, this is the first time that everything comes together. It is a defining moment … probably the most exciting part of the entire production process. The dubbing mixer ensures that all the sounds are at the right levels in relation to one another, the commentary can be heard clearly, the music does not intrude and the mood of the film is maintained. When it works, it can only be described as 'magic'.

SOUND RECORDING FOR FILM

THE EARLIEST WILDLIFE FILMS had no sound synchronized with the picture. Instead, there was a piano, a theatre organ or even an orchestra playing live in the cinema auditorium. But with the arrival of 'talkies', pictures had to have natural sound, bringing them another step closer to reality. The first microphones were relatively simple, capturing sound that was recorded first on wax cylinders and discs and later on magnetic tape. With more sophistication in picture gathering there was an upswing in sound recording too. The sound equivalents of the telephoto lens are the parabolic reflector or dish, a wok-shaped reflector with a microphone set at its focus point, and the gun microphone, a long, thin microphone with directional qualities. Recording natural sounds and atmospheres, however, differs from wildlife picture gathering in that it is difficult to cut out extraneous sounds, such as chainsaws, motorbikes and aircraft, so conditions have to be as near perfect as possible for sound recordists to obtain usable sound tracks. There are also specialized microphones for recording very high frequency sounds, such as those made by certain insects, and gadgets that shift the frequency of, say, the sounds made by bats, so that their calls and echolocation become audible to humans. Underwater recordings use specialized hydrophones, although a simple, tried-and-tested method is to place a standard microphone inside a condom to make it waterproof. It works perfectly!

A fringe-lipped bat homes in on the sound emitted by a frog in The Bat that Cracked the Frog Code, *an edition of* Wildlife on One.

[CHAPTER FIVE]

Getting There

When the film crew step out at the airport, luggage intact and cleared, the real fun begins. This is because the locations for wildlife films are rarely in the city in which the crew have just landed. They are out there, somewhere in the wilderness; onward travel may be by horse, camel, yak, donkey, dugout, ox cart, skidoo, helicopter, hydrofoil, river steamer, ice-breaker – in fact, just about any form of transport that you can imagine – and the journey can go on for ever. ☞

Above: Martin Saunders on location for Wildlife Special: Polar Bear.

A Different Kind of Travel Experience

It was a seemingly endless journey that producer Nigel Pope, zoologist and presenter Charlotte Uhlenbroek and cameraman Gavin Thurston undertook when heading into the interior of the Central African Republic in search of gorillas and forest elephants for *Secret Gorillas of Mondika*. It involved a seven-hour scheduled flight, three hours in a light aircraft, a six-hour river journey by dugout canoe and an eight-hour hike through the jungle ... at least it would have done had everything gone right.

'Things started to go wrong at the airport,' Nigel remembers, 'when we had one of those moments everyone dreads – a bag fails to turn up. The bag that was missing was the one containing all of Charlotte's clothes, and this town turned out to be a place that was not geared towards Westernized shopping for women. We had to find clothes suitable for the filming. The only bra she could get was an elaborate thing with sequins all over it, and outsized pants, so we teased her mercilessly. We packed it all up in a new rucksack and went off on this ludicrous journey.

'We were totally reliant on the dugout, simply a hollowed-out log with an outboard. The guides would stand in strategic positions with their feet blocking leaks, but even so there was always a few inches of water in the bottom. The engines were unreliable. We were 15 minutes into the journey when the engine stopped and we started to drift downstream, heading for the main river – the Congo. After a while, this man appeared in another dugout and jumped on board. He took the motor apart, put it together again and we resumed our journey.

'On the way, we made contact with a chap who was taking hunters into the jungle, and he knew some kind of local mafia chap who lived on the border of the Central African Republic who would pick up Charlotte's rucksack from a subsequent flight and transport it upriver to a bunch of local pygmies, who would then trek it into the jungle and find us. Ironically, it was the day before we were due to return from this very remote research camp that the pygmies arrived carrying the missing rucksack.

'The other thing was that the satellite phone was faulty and conversations back to base in Bristol were rather garbled. One of the things that worried us was the fact

BARTON, *LIFE OF BIRDS*

'I discovered that the nearest helicopter to the location was one permanently stationed at Nome on the Alaskan mainland. It did mail duties for Inuit communities in the area.'

that a cook who had been there a year previously was in hospital with TB – we were concerned about the prospect of people transferring TB to the gorillas. Gavin's father happens to be a doctor, so he attempted to phone him to ask how contagious he felt TB might be in this circumstance. Unfortunately, the satellite phone was so faulty that the only part of the message that got through was the mention of TB. In the UK, everybody was galvanized into action, with a full evacuation planned, helicopters, the lot.'

While working on *The Life of Birds* in 1998, Miles Barton had to rely on a helicopter to get him to a remote island off the Alaskan coast to film spectacled eiders. It turned into a logistical marathon. The birds' summer breeding grounds were known to be in the Arctic, but until 1995 no one had known where they spent the winter. It was then that radio-telemetry revealed they were south of St Lawrence Island in the Bering Sea. Bill Larned, of the US Fish and Wildlife Service, thought this must be a mistake and went by light aircraft to see for himself.

'He found the birds and took stills,' recalls Miles, 'and he showed us some remarkable pictures, so we decided we had to try to film this wildlife spectacle that had never been filmed before as an example of the ability of birds to endure the harshest of conditions. Easier said than done.

'I discovered that the nearest helicopter to the location was one permanently stationed at Nome on the Alaskan mainland. It did mail duties for Inuit communities in the area. This was less expensive than bringing one hundreds of miles from Anchorage, but it could not reach the location without refuelling on St Lawrence

Cameraman Ian McCarthy filming a wandering albatross chick in South Georgia for Life in the Freezer.

Island. So fuel had to be specially flown there in advance by charter plane. Cameraman David Rasmussen then had to wait for a week at Nome for the right weather conditions and when things improved he flew in the helicopter to St Lawrence Island. The pilot would not stop the rotors spinning in case they froze, so they loaded up and removed the door for filming while the blades were turning. The journey took over an hour, flying at speeds of 100 mph with the door off, so it was exceedingly cold. They finally reached the birds, but only had enough fuel to film for an hour before having to turn back. It was so cold that when David tried to film at high speed the film broke in the magazines. But again, it was all worth it, for out of the film that did stay in one piece we got an amazing sequence of the birds on the polynia – an area of open water within the sea ice.'

Helicopters, of course, can also be used to ferry kit and people from one inconvenient place to another. On a field trip for *The Living Isles* in 1986, producer Peter Crawford had to use one to take him and the film crew to and from a lighthouse on the Skelligs, off the west coast of Ireland. The gannets were spectacular and the filming went well, but when the helicopter came to take them back to the mainland things began to go wrong.

'We hit a very heavy rainstorm and suddenly there was a white-out at the front of the helicopter. The windshield wiper had spun off, so we could see nothing. The pilot, who was Irish, said, "Peter, could you look out on the left-hand side and see if there's anything down below?" The rain was lashing down and the wind blowing. The sound recordist was throwing up in the back and we couldn't see a thing. So I opened the window and looked down, and there were wires and cables and pylons everywhere. To cut a long story short, with the pilot looking out one side and me the other, we manoeuvred our way down to land safely in a field. I walked across to this farmhouse to be greeted by a very surprised but very hospitable Irish lady who said, "Ah, well now, it's good of you to drop in!"'

Another mode of transport is the light aircraft, and many wildlife filmmakers have experienced the gut-wrenching aeronautics of bush pilots in rickety planes. They seem to remain airborne by a wing and a prayer, but often there is no choice: this is the only form of local transport that can get into a remote area or the only craft available for aerial filming. When Peter Crawford had to go from Philadelphia to Delaware Bay to catch up with migrating snow geese for *Land of the Eagle* in 1990, he had to make a short hop in such a plane:

'I arrived in Philadelphia having come from San Francisco, and to get to the destination by dawn the following day, the guy who was going to do the aerial filming arranged to pick me up. He was waiting kindly at the reception where my plane dropped me off. He was a big chap, and he had with him his co-pilot, George, who turned out to be 68 and a crop sprayer. It was George who would be doing the flying with us the following day, but he had never flown in or out of an airport, just in and out of a field, so his colleague – the owner of the company – had come with him. I was piled into the back and they hadn't realized I'd have a lot of luggage with me. It was a very small plane and they were very big guys, so what with my luggage I made up quite a bit of weight as well. I had my barrel bags on my knees instead of in the compartment in the back and when I asked why, he said, "It's the only way we're going to get off the ground."

'So we approached the control tower and they said, "This is Cessna 232 calling for permission to go to 2000 feet." The tower came back – it was a very stern female controller – "Cessna 232, come a little closer, I can't read you." We drove right up to the tower and the girl in the tower opened the window and George the co-pilot opened his window and they shouted to each other. Permission was granted to fly at 1500 feet down south to Delaware Bay and we should now go and cross the main runway. So there we were heading for the main runway and George turned to his boss – neither of them had headphones, the radio was coming out of a squawk box – and said, "What'd ee say?" "She said go up to the main runway." So George goes up to the runway. There was this shaking feeling as he put the brakes on, then the voice came through the box again, saying something quite incomprehensible, and George said, "What'd ee say?" and the boss said, "George, go like hell!" He took the brakes off and I remember shooting across the main runway at Philadelphia – to my right there was a jumbo having landed and to my left were the lights of the next one coming in and I thought, "Pete, do you really need to do this?" But once we were up to 1500 feet and heading down south to Delaware Bay and the snow geese we were about to film, somehow you forget about all that.'

When producer Mike Salisbury was in the Canadian Arctic with cameraman Hugh Miles, filming *Kingdom of the Ice Bear*, their first trip was also by light aircraft:

'Our very first trip on paper read: fly to Yellowknife, the most northerly town in the Northwest Territories in Canada, hire a small plane, find the caribou and film them coming out of the trees. This was in late February and early March. We knew that the herd was about 100,000 animals, so we didn't think it was going to be very difficult to find, but the inevitable happened. We got to Yellowknife and were hit by the cold, and the scientist said, "Sorry, fellas, this is the first time that we haven't been able to find the caribou. We don't know where they are." So we hired this light aircraft and set off across the vast "land of the little sticks", as the Inuit call it – the scrubby edge of the treeline – looking for caribou. We spent three depressing days flying up and down with not a sign of any animals anywhere and we were thinking, "This is only our first trip – what have we undertaken?" We were also struck by the vastness of the place. It's fine when you're looking on a map, but when we were flying over it we realized we were looking for this group of caribou in an area the size of Wales.

'Eventually, on about the fourth day, we did see signs of thousands of animals having passed. The only thing then was to decide which way they had gone. It was a 50–50 chance we followed the right direction, but we found the straggling remains of the backmarkers. For the first time for many years, the herd had headed out on to the tundra about a month before they normally do, which is why we hadn't found them in the treeline.

'The little Cessna was on skis for the winter, and we said, "The caribou are down there, let's land somewhere the other side of that ridge and we'll climb up and film them from the top." The pilot said, "Oh, look, that looks like a smoothish patch; that's probably a frozen lake under that snow." So he came down to land and it was the roughest landing I've ever done in my life. All the film boxes hit the roof and we were bouncing around. I thought the little aircraft was going to totally break up and I turned to Jeff, the young pilot, and said, "Are landings on skis always as rough as this?" He said, "Aw, I don't know, it's the first one I've ever made myself."

'Getting off again was the same – warning lights were flashing, stall lights flashing and we hit the side of a drift of snow – it was rock hard and we bounced up into the air – it was a very dodgy moment!'

Small Boats and Snowmobiles

When filming in the Arctic, dodgy moments are not unusual and there were times when Mike Salisbury and Hugh Miles were in real danger. In Svarlbad in the Norwegian Arctic, their main mode of transport was the skidoo or snowmobile and Hugh was not enamoured of them:

'They were often covered in snow, but starting them in the morning was a horrible task. While Mike was cooking the breakfast, I'd go to try and pull-start the thing, and it would be 20 minutes on each skidoo to get the engine going. The cold air would really rasp your throat, so you'd have to dash in, have a quick sip of tea and carry on trying to get this damn skidoo going before we could go filming … and this was in the dark.'

Once going, the skidoos were the most efficient way to get from base to filming locations, but on one occasion things did not go as planned. Mike Salisbury takes up the story:

'I suppose the most dangerous occasion for me was when, looking for polar bear dens, my Norwegian guide got himself on to the side of a valley, which was almost sheet ice. The snow had blown off and underneath was a glazing of ice.

Cameraman Doug Allan drives a skidoo at Baffin Island in the Canadian Arctic.

His snowmobile started sliding down sideways and he was about to jump off, but the slope became steeper and steeper and disappeared into a sort of bottomless valley. It eventually stuck on a little rock sticking up out of the snow, but enough to stop him, and it was then a question of trying to pull him out. He had a long rope and I fixed that to his snowmobile. All the time, you had to use an ice axe to stop yourself from slipping down this slope, as we attached the rope. I got my snowmobile on to a better patch of snow higher up and, on the signal, he revved up and I revved up and I was just beginning to think I'd pulled him out when I hit a similar patch of glazed ice and started to swing like a pendulum on the end of this rope. My snowmobile started to slip down the same slope sideways and hit a little patch of stones and turned over. I saw sky-snow-sky-snow and wondered what on earth was going to happen. I grappled to stay on the slope, and the snowmobile kept on going for a few yards and eventually landed the right way up and stuck on some rocks. We looked at each other from a distance. I put my thumbs up and we had to go through the whole procedure again. Luckily the snowmobile wasn't too damaged, but it really was a frightening moment. Nobody would have been able to find us. It suddenly brought home to me the smallness of human beings in that vast wilderness. It was a moment of humility, actually.'

Small boats are another obvious hazard and using them to get to islands, especially those in the open ocean, is especially dangerous. For one thing, remote islands are notoriously difficult to land on. During the making of *Atlantic Realm*, producer Steve Nichols had to take more than his fair share of risks:

'The one where I began to think, "Is this really sensible?" was filming on Boatswain Bird Island, a small islet off the east coast of Ascension in the South Atlantic where there are large bird colonies. It's a pretty rough place on which to land. There's just a rope dangling off a cliff, which you grab on to from the boat and haul yourself up about 20 feet to a small concrete landing stage. From there it's a climb and scramble to the top. It's hard to land there, anyway, because there's a big sea running – a 20–30-foot swell. We had to take the gear in a larger boat from Ascension and transfer it to a smaller boat to land, and then get it all on to this landing stage. We then had to climb to the top and it was all guano, crumbly bird droppings that got into the eyes and throat. No one had been there for six or seven years, so we were using this rope that we hadn't a clue whether it was worn at the top and we had to rely on it to get up the cliff face. You couldn't use handholds, as they were full of nesting birds. I was halfway up the slope with cameraman Mike Potts when I looked down and we could see that the channel between Boatswain Bird and Ascension was absolutely full of sharks. We thought, "Well, this is great –

Film crew on skidoos looking for polar bears at Admiralty Inlet in the Canadian Arctic.

we're hanging on a rope we don't know is safe, dangling over shark-infested waters and there's nothing much else to hang on to." We struggled on and it was worth it, for the top of the island was dramatic, with its nesting boobies and frigate birds, but there were times when we thought otherwise.'

When David Attenborough travelled for the first time to the Indonesian island of Komodo to film its giant monitor lizards for *Zoo Quest*, the authorities did not know they existed. The only form of transport available was a local fishing boat, but the owner seemed to know less about where they were heading than the film crew did.

'He put us on a coral reef a couple of times,' recalls Attenborough, 'and then we discovered he wasn't a sailor at all and these weren't his waters. He was actually a gunrunner on the run from the Indonesian authorities. So we took over the navigation, but that was not all that sensible because all we had was a map out of an airline's in-flight magazine on which the island of Komodo was the size of a full stop. We got into some frightful scrapes, in whirlpools and one thing and another, and finally landed on the island. But when we came to sail back, the local chief said, "The captain you've got is not a good man ... he said to us you've got a lot of money and a lot of equipment and he could take it from you ... so watch out." So, all the way back, Charles [Lagus, the cameraman] and I didn't sleep at the same time. It was the first time the dragons had been filmed and the trip took a couple of weeks. When I went back for *The Living Planet* [nearly 30 years later], it took less than a couple of days.'

Stepping into Things

It was on an expedition for *The Living Planet* that David Attenborough found himself heading out across the northern Sahara Desert to film ancient rock art in the Tassili Mountains. The trip was organized by the series production manager (who in BBC parlance was then called 'organizer'), Andrew Buchanan. At that time, the series had the working title *Planet Earth*, so Andrew had the rather majestic title 'Organizer: Planet Earth'. Part of his duties was to arrange transport across the desert, but he was adamant that the only way was on foot, with the equipment carried on donkeys. Nothing else was available or capable of making such a journey. So the team set out across the rocky terrain, each person following in the footsteps of the one in front. After a while, with the sun blazing down from a cloudless sky and no shade anywhere, Attenborough noticed the unmistakable outline of a car tyre. 'Why are we walking,' he thought, 'when we could be driving?' He said nothing and continued along the trail, but then saw more tyre marks in the sand ... and this went on all the way to the first night's camp. By this time, he was a bit annoyed and was just about to remonstrate with Andrew when he looked down. As the organizer sat down by the campfire and stretched out his tired legs, the mystery became clear. Being a practical conservationist and recycler, Andrew was wearing sandals with the soles made from old car tyres!

On foot might sound a reasonably harmless way to get to and from work, but it does, of course, depend on where the route takes you. Cameraman Roger Jackman's walk to work in Sarawak, for an edition of *Natural World*, is one that he remembers with less than fond memories:

'One of the sequences was in a huge cave. It had an entrance 400 feet tall and 60 feet wide, and the whole mountain was hollow. It got even bigger inside, and in one of the caverns lived a population of about five million bats. Each day we were filming there, we had a choice of route – the short route that went over the top of a huge pile of guano or the long route over big stones and past chasms where it was easy to slip in the dark and which was three times as long. So the short route became the favoured option. The only thing was that at the top of the guano heap were thousands of very large earwigs, each about half an inch long, and they had the delightful habit of living off the dead skin of bats. Many of them, of course, fell off and their instinct was to get back up again and make for the highest point. Our short route took us over the highest point. As it was a slow process getting through, we were absolutely covered in these things. You might have a hundred or two hundred on you, which had crawled up under your ears, inside your shirt, under your arms; and if you left the bottoms of your trousers open, they'd certainly have been up there. At the end of the day's filming, we'd rush down the guano mound and into the river to get rid of them. It was quite disgusting.'

ALDRICH-BLAKE, *WILDLIFE ON ONE*

'There was a roost that was said to have a half a million bats, and underneath it was an enormous pile of bat guano and the whole surface was shimmering and seething with golden cockroaches.'

Producer Pelham Aldrich-Blake found himself in a similar cave system when filming cave swiftlets in Gomantong Caves in Sabah, Borneo, for *Wildlife on One: Serpents, Swiftlets and the Chasm of Gloom*. These are the birds that make the nests for birds' nest soup, but it was the bats that made the cave a very unpleasant place to be.

'Some of the toughest filming was done on the floor of the cave. As well as cave swiftlets, there were enormous numbers of bats and where you get bats you get bat droppings. There was a roost that was said to have a half a million bats, and underneath it was an enormous pile of bat guano and the whole surface was shimmering and seething with golden cockroaches. We had to get to the top of this mound to film the bats in their roost. It was like climbing up a sand dune, and as you climbed increasingly more cockroaches climbed on to you and scrambled up to the top of your head. As you got gradually higher, so the stench of ammonia became more pronounced. When right at the top you could hardly breathe. Of course, all the bats were disturbed, so a few tens of thousands of them were swirling round you as well. That was the one occasion when I did begin to wonder whether this was a very good idea after all. And if that wasn't enough, there were parts of the cave where, just as on the seashore you might get quicksand, you found 'quick-guano'. Any depression in the cave floor filled up with water and bat droppings, so you'd get a hard crust on top but underneath it was liquid. One heard stories of people walking into these evil-smelling swamps and disappearing without trace. I did on one occasion go in up to my waist and managed to scramble out again, but it was a disconcerting moment.'

Gomantong's guano heap was the location for a sequence in the cave episode of the recent *Planet Earth* series. The guano was just as high and just as unpleasant, but the stakes had risen too. The film crew had to get new angles on familiar animals and they were shooting on high-definition video – a whole new cave experience. Learning from their predecessors, the team adopted paper suits as protection, but the cockroaches still dropped down their necks, and any split that was not sealed up with gaffer tape let in the creeping and crawling hordes. The humidity and temperature were such that the electronic camera malfunctioned regularly and the cable dolly (see Chapter Seven) was such a Heath Robinson contraption that it kept breaking down. Nevertheless the crew obtained their shots and the hardships involved in getting them are long forgotten.

Borneo's caves seem to have featured in more travellers' tales than most locations. They are just so unpleasant, they stick in people's memories. Barry Paine is another producer who has a tale about them:

'We were filming in some enormous caves on Mount Mulu and we'd finished for the day, but when we came out the weather was overcast, prelude to a tropical downpour. It was late afternoon and we had five miles of hard walking through the forest, followed by a long boat trip. We set off, but had underestimated the force of the storm. It was also getting dark, but we had our local guides and we were following a well-worn path. Every now and then we had to cross a river. They had been dry streambeds when we came that way in the morning, but every one we came to in the evening was running a little stronger and a little deeper. The first was up to our knees, the next up to our thighs and the cameraman Hugh Maynard turned to me and said, "Barry, you really get me into some fixes."

'The next river was chest deep, and as we were not carrying equipment we were lighter than the porters. They each had a box of equipment on their heads, which seemed to keep them from floating away. We came to one river that was flowing quite fiercely and I suddenly realized that my feet had lost contact with the ground. I had a torch in one hand and I was floating off down this river in the dark; I remember the thought going through my mind, "I wonder what I put on the next-of-kin form!"

'Fortunately, my feet found a pile of shingle and I could get a grip, so I just lodged there with the rest of me completely under water and I'm glad to say that the porters and the rest of the party came down the bank a little way, looked into the water and pulled me out. But that wasn't the end of the tale. We went on down the path, somewhat chastened by the experience, and eventually we reached the longboat. The main river, by then, had swollen considerably. A tree had been washed across and we had to get the longboat over it before we could continue our journey. We had to push it up over the tree and then have somebody in the prow to weight it down so it would slide into the river on the other side. I volunteered to go into the front. They pushed it up and the boat tipped. The bow went into the river and I thought it would float, but it went down and kept on going, so I went under. After what felt like a long time, it came up and was back in the air – my second dunking of the day. When we arrived finally at the camp, there was a party going on in the longhouse and we were welcomed back as if nothing had happened.'

On another occasion, Barry Paine was in the wonderful cloud forest of Monteverde in Costa Rica when he was caught not only in more torrential rain, but also in the mother of all electrical storms:

'We were high on a very exposed ridge. We dived back into the forest and followed this path down at a rate of knots and the guide kept saying, "Señor, señor, this is very dangerous." I could really appreciate this, because the lightning was ripping into the forest, thankfully some distance away, but you could hear ominous crackling noises when it happened. The thunder was ear-splitting, and thunder and lightning were happening at the same time. The guide said, "Señor, señor, come quick, but if you feel the hair stand up on the back of your neck, throw yourself in the mud." Well, being British, I had no intention of throwing myself in the mud … but we did run!'

Temporary Homes and Unexpected Visitors

Returning each evening, covered in mud, dust or cockroaches, wet right through from a tropical downpour or frozen stiff from sitting in a hide in the snow, the wildlife film-maker's temporary home is often a blessed relief. Crews eat and sleep in the most extraordinary places, ranging from luxury hotels to the varying degrees of discomfort of tents on land, tents on ice, mud houses, tree houses, houseboats, flimsy plywood huts, igloos, refuges made of rocks, even under the stars. On one of their first shoots in the Norwegian Arctic for *Kingdom of the Ice Bear*, Mike Salisbury and Hugh Miles were camped out on the sea ice.

'We'd both been lying awake in this tent,' Mike says. 'The Norwegians were in the next tent and both myself and Hugh had been hearing this crunching and creaking noise. Hugh whispered to me, "Did you hear that noise?" and I said, "Yes, you don't think it's a polar bear, do you?" Hugh said, "I'm just beginning to wonder that myself" and we lay there – crunch, creak ... and our hearts pounding. You feel very vulnerable with just a little layer of canvas between you and the outside. The Norwegians must have heard the same noise, because one of them eventually called out, "Don't worry, I think it's just the ice cracking underneath the tent," and we said, "Oh, that's all right, then" and went to sleep. Which just shows that your level of fear depends on what you're afraid of, because normally I'd have been very afraid of ice cracking underneath me. A polar bear seemed worse and actually, when we looked in the morning, there were polar bear tracks all around us.

'Wherever we camped, we stuck posts around the tent and we had wires stretched between the posts. On each post was an explosive device with a pin on it. If a polar bear touched the wire, the pin would come out and bang, it would send this flare up into the sky. The bang would scare the bear away and the flare would light up the sky so you'd be able to see what on earth was going on. The only trouble was that if you went out to relieve yourself in the middle of the night, you'd trip over the wire and the whole shooting match would go up!'

Out on the Arctic sea ice, those simple things of life become major events, as *Wildlife Special: Polar Bear* producer Martha Holmes discovered:

'Living conditions in the Arctic are such that every time you want to go for a pee, you have to take a gun or a flare. You have to tell somebody what you're doing, just in case you don't come back or there's a polar bear waiting there.'

But it was not during any of those vulnerable moments that any bears turned up. They waited until Martha and her guides had gone to bed. She had wanted to set up a tripwire, but the Inuit guides, behaving rather macho in front of a young woman, laughed it off, saying, 'Don't be so silly, we've been camping here for years with no problems.' Earlier in the day, however, the guides had caught a seal and the smell of seal meat was wafting out on the breeze, an open invitation to polar bears.

'The first I knew about it was crunch, crunch, crunch on the gravel outside my tent,' says Martha. 'I thought at first it was one of the guys going for a pee, but it was rather close. Then I heard this heavy breathing. I knew it was a polar bear. I was in

Above: Hugh Miles waiting to film polar bear cubs on location for Kingdom of the Ice Bear.

Right: Cameraman Doug Allan and an Inuit guide film a swimming polar bear from an ice floe for Wildlife Special: Polar Bear.

a tent on my own, so I lay there and then I heard the sound go around to the front of my tent. It didn't sound weighty enough for a big bear, so I sat up and slowly unzipped my tent so there was a small hole to look out. As I peeked out, this tiny polar bear cub was peeking in and I thought, "Heck, mother must be around somewhere." I heard the mother in the kitchen area, looking for the dead seal, so I whispered to the guides, "There's a bear in camp." No response, so I whispered louder, "There's a bear in camp" and even louder, "*Get up, there's a bear in camp!*" It was like some farce, with arms and legs moving in all directions as the three guys came out of their deep sleep. Fortunately, the mother bear gathered up her two cubs and ran off.

'But that wasn't the end of it. I woke up an hour later to the sound of growling and canvas ripping. The bear had come back to get the seal meat. I just lay there, flat for five minutes, avoiding the bullets that were flying about and with the prospect of a bear rampaging through the tent. Apparently the bear had returned, tripped over a guy rope and slashed out in anger. It went through the guys' tent and they started shooting.'

Martha survived the bear and the bullets, and so did three very embarrassed Inuit guides. The persistence of polar bears, though, is well known to Arctic veterans and

can often give cause for concern. When *Planet Earth* cameraman Doug Allan and field assistant Jason Roberts were in the Norwegian Arctic, they had a similar experience, the difference being that they were in a wooden hut. They were preparing the evening meal when Doug heard a noise. There was a bear outside, and a big one too – a large male that had probably picked up the smell of cooking and was determined to get in. It explored the door, then put its face to the window and could easily have broken in, but Jason fired a gun and Doug threw out a thunderflash. The bear did not budge and began chewing on the generator cable in frustration. More thunderflashes and a flare eventually encouraged it to back off, but it was a close thing.

While polar bears are a constant hazard in the Arctic, the same is true of lions on the East African savannah. They are often active at night and can scare the heck out of the unwary. On one occasion, Barry Paine was in the Serengeti making *The World About Us: Kopje: A Rock for all Seasons*, a film about the blocks of granite – 'islands in a sea of grass' – that thrust up through the volcanic ash of those vast plains. The crew had their tents arranged next to one of the kopjes and at three o'clock one morning Barry woke up with a start to the sound of something rubbing along the side of his tent.

'I thought it was somebody pushing past, but couldn't understand who it would be. Then, about ten minutes later, a male lion began that magnificent call, the personification of Africa, I think – that great, deep, throaty roar. It's an extraordinary sound and quite terrifying when it's only about 12 feet away from you. It shakes the ground, and it shakes you, and by then you're wide awake. I was sitting on the edge of the bed thinking, "What happens now?" You are told not to go out of the tent, so you have to stay inside. You can't see what's outside and the sound grows in your mind. I thought, "If I just go back to bed and pull the covers over my head, it'll all be fine in the morning." So I tried that, but there's no way you can lie on a camp bed with the covers over your head and listen to that sound. I was up again, on the edge of the bed and the hair was standing up on the back of my neck, and you think, "I am afraid!" And you *are* afraid – you feel real gut fear. It's as afraid as I ever wish to be, and I felt desperately alone. Then a small voice called out, "Barry, he's nearer to you than he is to us," and suddenly that fear was broken by the sense that you weren't alone. They had all been listening and we all laughed at once, and somehow the whole situation seemed to be far less fearful.'

Rattlesnake, Armadillo and Other Delicacies

Night-time encounters can involve the most unexpected animals. When making *An Island Called Danger,* on the Indian Ocean island of that name, Peter Crawford was camping out with the eminent botanist and broadcaster David Bellamy. One of the island's more unusual residents is a large land crab – the coconut crab, which climbs trees – and this was almost Professor Bellamy's undoing.

'David and I were sharing a tent,' recalls Peter, 'and he woke up in the middle of the night and said, "Hey, Pete, do you think you could help?" I got out my torch and shone it on David. He was lying on his back, and around his beard he had the claws of a land crab. They're big animals, about a foot and a half across the shell, but with a little bit of encouragement the crab released its grip on David's beard and throat. I'm afraid the crab didn't come out of it too well. The following day, we ate it.'

Food is whatever the camp chef can acquire, usually served with rice, and to the filmmakers' horror the star of the day's filming is sometimes served up for supper. Just about every animal family has been represented on the dinner plate at one time or another, so the location cookbook can contain all manner of unusual recipes, as producer Robin Prytherch can verify:

'They said, "We've got a good meal for you tonight," and I sat down to this amazing meal of rattlesnake, armadillo and grits (a southern vegetable dish with rice). The armadillo was like very rich pork and the snake was like chicken.'

The star of the day's filming is sometimes served up for supper. Just about every animal family has been on the dinner plate at one time or another, so the location cookbook can contain all manner of unusual recipes

The food, though, is not always to everybody's liking. During one trip to Japan producer Miles Barton was presented with a dish that resembled frogspawn, but turned out to be fermented bean sprouts, followed by an extraordinary fish dish:

'I'm not keen on fish at the best of times, but they gave me a slice of fish which looked like cold meat with a circle of yellow paste in the middle, rather like that sweet bread you used to get with marzipan running through it. Anyway, the smell and taste were almost indescribable – rotting fish, stale feet and mouldy cheese with a touch of ammonia. It turned out that this delicacy is prepared by taking gravid fish, with the eggs still inside, and burying them underground to rot for six months. Then salt is added and they're sliced. The yellow "marzipan" was fermented fish roe. I had to swallow it or offend my hosts!'

The evening meal, of course, can be a time when local folk want to entertain their visitors; to refuse their hospitality would at best be offensive and at worst bring an abrupt end to filming. Martin Saunders discovered this while filming *Kingdom of the Ice Bear*. His Inuit guides had just shot a seal and he was offered the still-warm liver. The Inuit consider this a great delicacy and it would have been rude not to accept the raw offering.

'He gave it to us on the blade of a knife,' recalls Martin, 'and it was warm and pulsing, and actually it tasted delicious.'

A celebratory feast in Mongolia was something of a challenge for Martha Holmes. For starters, the sheep at the centre of the meal was killed in an unexpected way. A slit was cut in its chest and the slaughterman pushed his hand inside and squeezed the heart until it was dead. This method of killing made sure that all the blood was inside, with nothing wasted. The sheep was then cut up and put in a cauldron to make 'five-important-organ soup', but to Martha's astonishment everything went into the pot. Eyes, intestines and bits of brain bubbled to the surface of the grey broth – and she too had to eat it or cause great offence.

Producer Peter Crawford can go one better. He was in Indonesia, making a costume drama about the explorer and naturalist Alfred Russell Wallace. Before arriving at the location in Borneo, it was suggested that the local village folk would appreciate a present or two as a token of friendship.

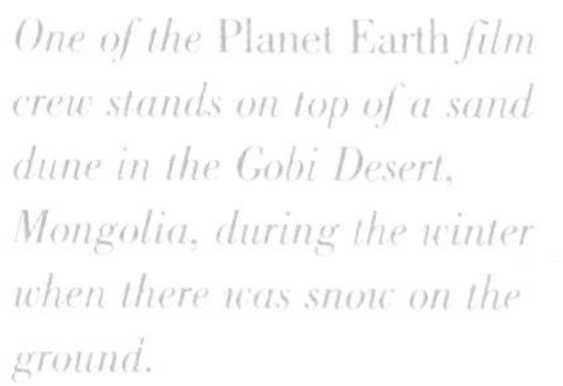

One of the Planet Earth *film crew stands on top of a sand dune in the Gobi Desert, Mongolia, during the winter when there was snow on the ground.*

'They said a case of brandy would go down well with the men, and the many families living in the two longhouses would appreciate some fresh meat. As they're not Muslim, pork would be fine. So since we didn't have a fridge, a live porker was bought in the market and transported in a suitably made cage. The pig as a present went down well but, to appease the gods before we could start filming, the big white chief – the producer of the programme – would have to kill the pig, and I had to do it by driving a stake through the jugular. "Is this absolutely necessary?" I asked the interpreter and he said, "I'll give you this tip – if you don't, you won't be allowed to film." So in front of everybody, I had to dispatch this pig. Fortunately, having been brought up on a farm in Sussex, I knew a little about slaughtering. However, it was not something I'd ever done, and not something I'd want to do again, but the pig died quickly and the spirits were appeased.'

Spirits of a different kind can also be important in lubricating relations, and things can get out of hand. Miles Barton was in West Africa to film fruit bats when he had to offer a 'libation' of strong spirits to the local chief. The village elder then appeased the ancestors by pouring some on the floor and shared the rest with the film crew:

'This was 40-degree-proof white spirit, and at ten o'clock in the morning it wasn't conducive to an efficient day's filming.'

But this was nothing compared to another drinking bout Miles had to undergo in China, where he was to film snub-nosed monkeys for *Cousins*. The crew had travelled through the night with no lights along a switchback road, to arrive exhausted at seven o'clock in the morning. They had been sleeping for about three hours when they were woken up and asked to go for a meeting with the park manager:

'That's when the toasting started. They served mead – the local delicacy – and after a few our interpreter told me the custom was to drink the health of everyone at the table – about 20 people. After the first five, I was trying to take sips, but they wouldn't let me get away with that. After ten, I was trying to refuse as politely as possible a jovial individual who was waving his glass at me. I told the interpreter that I really couldn't drink any more, but he told me I had to.

'"Why?" I asked.

'"Because he's the chief of police, that's why!" So I did.'

Almost everyone travelling and filming overseas has had to endure the local specialities at one time or another, yet surprisingly few get sick. There is the odd case of 'Delhi belly', but wildlife filmmakers in the main seem to have cast-iron stomachs. There was, however, a regular member of the NHU's film crews who resolutely refused to eat the local food, whatever was served up. His suitcase was filled not with a change of clothes, but with tins of a well-known brand of creamed rice.

KEEPING FROM BEING SEEN

THERE ARE FEW PLACES on this planet – mostly remote, uninhabited islands – where wild animals are not wary of people, so cameramen and camerawomen must conceal or camouflage themselves in order not to frighten their subjects away. The most convenient hide or blind is a car. On the savannahs of East Africa, for instance, wildlife completely ignore cars and their passengers, so the four-wheel-drive vehicle is the ideal camera platform. During the filming of *Big Cat Diary*, the wildlife became so familiar with camera cars that cheetahs even used them as vantage points from which to scan the plains for prey.

Hides may be on precarious platforms near the top of 60-metre (200-foot) high rainforest trees or perched on the side of mountains and cliff faces, reachable only by ropes or rope ladders. In the Arctic, hides are made by building half-igloos of compacted snow. In order to film flamingos on East African lakes, ornithologist Leslie Brown devised a floating hide that, when entering or leaving the water, he could lift like somebody gathering up their skirt to go paddling.

Some photographers go to extraordinary lengths to make themselves invisible. In the early days, Oliver Pike disguised himself as a haystack in order to film a cuckoo at in a meadow pipit's nest; more recently two well-known wildlife presenters, quite independently, were disguised as a hedge in order to get close to kingfishers. The simple, square, cloth tent hide is still used to conceal the camera and its operator, but the subject has to be tricked into believing it is empty. Two people go in, but only one comes out. Wild animals, it seems, cannot count!

Above: Cameraman Richard Kirby films high in the rainforest in Sabah, Southeast Asia for The Private Life of Plants.

Right: A camouflaged tent used for filming hooded cranes in the far east of Russia.

[CHAPTER SIX]

Up Close and Dangerous

No matter how much research has been done and how often the time and place of an event has been checked out with scientists in the field, inevitably the film crew arrive on location to be greeted with the immortal words, 'Gosh, you should have been here yesterday.' Mother Nature can thwart even the best-laid plans. It is what makes wildlife filmmaking very different from other types ... well, that, and the waiting. Wildlife camera people have the patience of Job. ☞

Above: A mountain gorilla inspects its own image in the lens of a film camera in the Congo.

Patience Pays Off

The dedication that camerapeople have can be summed up by the story behind a single shot in *Planet Earth.* The programme wanted show a snow leopard, but it is a shy and retiring animal, notoriously difficult to find, let alone film, in the rugged mountains of Pakistan. Scientists trying to study it rarely get a sighting. Two previous attempts to film it had failed. As cameraman Doug Allan said, 'These are big, big mountains and there are not many snow leopards.' In an attempt to overcome the difficulties, Doug lived in a mountain refuge built of stones for several weeks, putting out camera traps at key crossing places, hoping to get the animals to film themselves, but the main way of working was the tried and tested one – just sit in a hide with the camera and wait. After seven weeks, Doug had managed a few fleeting shots of a distant snow leopard and the camera traps had taken some close-ups. The team then decided to take a gamble and try a new location, but the hunt for terrorists meant that only news crews had access to the mountains until the political situation stabilized. So that, for the time being, was that.

The dedication of the Planet Earth *team paid off when they captured on film a snow leopard and her cub at a cave.*

A year later, the team was allowed back into Pakistan, to film on the border with Afghanistan, but the trek in was difficult. Rockslides were common and football-sized boulders whizzed past at head height, but the presence of snow leopard scat confirmed that the animals were around. Doug Allan had been assigned elsewhere, so Mark Smith took over the daunting task, spending several weeks in winter, including Christmas, alone in a mountain refuge waiting for the big cat to appear. Finally, he had some luck: 'I looked up at the ridge and could see this leopard. It was perched on top of a rock and looked down at us. It just sat down in a sphinx-like posture.'

Mark's patience had paid off. He and the rest of the crew were able to spend two weeks with the snow leopard, and the sequence he filmed culminated in an extraordinary shot of it racing down the mountainside chasing a markhor (mountain goat) – a wild snow leopard hunt, something few humans have ever seen.

The NHU is fortunate in having had a long and productive relationship with the best wildlife cameramen and camerawomen in the world. It is the skill of these largely unsung heroes that makes or breaks a wildlife film: they are pushing the boundaries of what is possible all the time. The activities of some of the *Planet Earth* camera teams serve to illustrate the great diversity of environments in which they may find themselves, and the patience and ingenuity they must show in order to capture their subjects on film.

Ian McCarthy spent three weeks on a tuna trawler pushing against the roaring forties in order to reach an island from which seals launched attacks on penguins, and then braved four weeks of gales and aggressive bull fur seals to get the shots he wanted. Further south, a year in the Antarctic was the only way Wade Fairley and his partner Frédérique Olivier could film emperor penguins, including the extraordinarily dedicated parenting behaviour of the male birds in the dark and icy-cold depths of winter. Wade was battered by the worst weather on the planet, yet able to film behaviour, such as male birds squabbling, that was entirely new to science.

In New Guinea, the camera crew waited patiently for 45 days for a rare species of bird of paradise to perform its courtship display, while another crew waited for days in one spot in southern Russia for an Amur leopard to appear. Filming the migration of Mongolian gazelles – another phenomenon that few people have witnessed – took three years to achieve and even so nearly failed at the last moment. There is little cover on the steppe and the animals are so shy that the cameraman had to bury himself up to the neck in order not to be seen. A microlite was shipped from South America so that he could film from the air, but the machine was damaged and written off before a single frame was shot. Eventually, an ageing Russian helicopter carried the cameraman aloft and *Planet Earth* was furnished with unforgettable images of hundreds of gazelles on the move.

PLANET EARTH

It is the skill of these largely unsung heroes that makes or breaks a wildlife film: they are pushing the boundaries of what is possible all the time.

Pygmy hogs in tropical India proved a problem not because of the hogs themselves but because of the other animals in the area. These little porkers hide in tall jungle grass, which was problem enough in itself for the filmmakers, but the high concentration of tigers in the area added to the tension. While trekking on foot, however, among grass that grows higher than a person can jump, the main danger was from rhinos. The team had to put up with being charged almost every day before the pictures were in the can.

Dolphins that aquaplane on breakers along a beach in Western Australia proved an unexpected headache. Only a few of them exhibit this behaviour, so to determine where and when they would perform was almost impossible. The crew spent many hours running up and down baking hot sand dunes, carrying their heavy kit, in the often fruitless search for a surfer. A cooling dip in the sea was off limits due to an unusually large population of sharks.

The Polar Bears Emerge

Planet Earth had the good fortune and the finances to film all over the world, catching amazing behaviour wherever it went. This is an aspiration that has motivated wildlife filmmakers since the first hand-cranked film went through the gate all those years ago. And knowing when not to switch off the camera is as important as knowing when to switch it on. Martin Saunders was filming for *Realms of the Russian Bear* on Wrangel Island in the Russian Arctic when he came across an incredible sight. The winter ice had been late in forming, so a huge group of walruses was gathered on the beach and was being attacked by polar bears. Polar bears are enormous, but the walruses dwarfed them. Bears would clamber on to a walrus's back but be dislodged by a quick shake of its huge bulk. It was something that had never been seen before. Martin just pressed the trigger and kept it pressed until the film ran out or the polar bears lost interest.

During the making of *Kingdom of the Ice Bear*, Hugh Miles and Mike Salisbury were in Svarlbad, where polar bear mothers give birth in snow dens during the long, dark winter. Hugh and Mike wanted to be there at the moment when mother and cubs first emerged from the den in spring – behaviour that had never been filmed before, for the simple reasons that dens are difficult to find and predicting when a bear is going to emerge is well nigh impossible. Hugh tells how they fared in such a hostile environment:

MILES, *KINGDOM OF THE ICE BEAR*

'We were down to –46°C (–51°F) plus a wind chill that almost froze the flesh. You could do a shot for ten or twenty seconds and then had to turn away.'

'Having spoken to several scientists and explorers, who told us it was cold enough to kill us, we realized early on that we should do a survival course first, so we spent ten days in the Cairngorms in the middle of winter. We learned cross-country skiing, how to use ropes, ice axes and pitons, and how to slide down mountains on our back and not go over precipices. Then we went to see the Royal Marines and spoke to

Cameraman Doug Allan prepares to film polar bears in an air temperature of -25°C at Hopen Island, Norway.

them about clothing and some of the ways they avoid dying in the cold. So we felt pretty well equipped to face anything once we got to the Arctic. And we're glad we did it. We were down to –46°C (–51°F) plus a wind chill that almost froze the flesh. You could do a shot for ten or twenty seconds and then had to turn away.'

Even after they had found a den, Mike recalls that filming didn't go according to plan:

'We camped by one den and the female eventually came out. Hugh got some nice shots of her just sticking her head out and going back in. Eventually she came out and wandered down the valley. We looked in the den and found there were no cubs, so we'd been sitting by the one female in the whole of Svarlbad that had had a phantom pregnancy. We did really feel that our luck was running out.'

Food supplies and fuel were running out too, but they decided on one last search:

Hugh Miles filming moulting cinstrap penguins for Life in the Freezer.

'Hugh and Rasmuss [their local Norwegian guide] noticed a plug of snow up on a slope near the sea ice. They watched it and saw a very thin bear going back into the hole, so we assumed it was a den. We set about building a half-igloo to shield Hugh and his camera, and then we had to sit in the bitter cold and wait.'

It had been worth their wait. The female came out and slid down the slope before returning to her den. A couple of days later the first cub appeared, although Hugh was still hard pressed to get anything on film:

'The eyepiece iced up and so there are one or two shots, including the best-known shot of the mother sliding down with the cubs, where I could hardly see anything at all through the viewfinder. I had to pull-focus using instinct, keeping my left eye open to see if she was coming slightly closer and just crept the focus hoping that I got it sharp. I couldn't see anything through the camera, but I was thinking, "This is just great."'

What Hugh hadn't realized was that he was losing body heat fast. He was suffering from hypothermia and had to be revived with hot soup and a warm sleeping bag. The cold, however, was one thing; the ice bears were quite another. One swipe from a powerful forepaw could break a person's neck. Fieldcraft in this situation meant understanding how your subject was likely to behave.

'We got to know how they looked when they were dodgy. The ears and head would be a bit lower, and they generally looked a bit mean. There was one that kept following us and we fired a little flare to scare it away, but it kept on coming. The reason was we'd found a dead reindeer and strapped it to the back of the sledge. The bear had picked up the smell. At one stage it came up very fast and we leapt on our skidoos to get out of town, and the damn skidoo wouldn't start ... and this polar bear was closing on us.'

This wasn't their only close call. On another occasion they were strapping equipment to their sledge when an Arctic fox appeared. He had been visiting the camp every day for handouts and was especially fond of raisins. Suddenly he ran off, his tail between his legs.

'I turned around,' recalls Hugh, 'and there was this huge polar bear coming in to see what that action was. He was just a few yards behind us. I spun around and leapt over the sledges to get the rifle and Mike dived into the tent to get a thunderflash. We threw the thunderflash, but the bear was already running away over the ice, his great white bottom waddling away in the distance. It was an amusing incident really, but if our fox hadn't have been there, the bear would have been on us, I guess without us even noticing ... It could have been pretty nasty.'

Piranhas and Other Perils

Piranhas are pretty nasty too; at least so we are led to believe. Cameraman Peter Scoones and producer Mark Brownlow went in search of them in the Pantanal in Brazil for the freshwater episode of *Planet Earth* and, despite the confidence of their local piranha-expert guide, they spent several fruitless days diving in coffee-coloured water with no sign of the fish. After surveying vast tracks of wetland from a spotter plane, looking for suitable habitat, they came to a place where the local fishermen were catching piranhas to eat. Many of the men had scars where the fish had bitten them. But when Peter did finally dive with piranhas they shied away from him. He tried diving at night, to no avail. Eventually, two weeks after they started searching, they found feeding piranhas in clear water. Peter got his shots of a feeding frenzy, but was not attacked once.

About a year later, producer James Brickell, working on the new Attenborough series *Life in Cold Blood*, was not so lucky. He was in Argentina to film anacondas

Above: A Planet Earth *film crew travels through Brazil's Pantanal, the largest wetland habitat in the world.*

Right: Cameramen Peter Scoones and Doug Anderson film feeding piranha for Planet Earth.

and was in a small boat with the rest of the crew during the heat of the day. To help cool off as the boat drifted along, they let their hands dangle in the water. Suddenly James felt a jolt and, thinking it was the guide playing a trick, turned to look, but the man was too far away. Taking his hand out of the water, James found that a piranha had taken off the top of his finger. They *are* dangerous after all.

Being attacked by animals in the wild is a rare occurrence. Wildlife filmmakers pride themselves on their ability to detect when an animal is stressed or likely to become aggressive. A slow, tactical withdrawal usually avoids any danger, but just occasionally things go awry, as when Nigel Pope was filming in the Central African

Republic with presenter Charlotte Uhlenbroek and cameraman Gavin Thurston. They had set up an ambitious shot in a clearing frequented by lowland gorillas and forest elephants. Charlotte was with the elephant expert and two pygmy trackers on one side of the clearing; Nigel and Gavin were with the camera on an observational platform on the other. Nigel remembers:

'It was a great opportunity to get a shot with a presenter at the back and the animals in the foreground. Everybody was in place and so we waited for elephants to arrive. Charlotte had a walkie-talkie with which we could communicate with her and we had a nice shot lined up with some passing elephants, especially a mother with a baby. I cued her on the walkie-talkie and the mother elephant must have picked up the noise – to my horror I saw Charlotte sprinting up the hill with the elephant in hot pursuit. Forest elephants are particularly nasty. They have tusks that curve downwards with which they can skewer you on the ground. Charlotte made it to where the researcher and guide were hiding, ducked behind a tree and the elephant backed away. We thought that was it – they'd had their warning – but then the elephant came in for a second charge. You knew it meant business. It was out to get them. It was only at the last minute that the two pygmy guides – small in stature but really tough – leapt out into the path of the charging elephant and started to stone it with rocks, and they stood their ground until it backed off – a terrifying experience.'

Being attacked by animals in the wild is a rare occurrence. Filmmakers pride themselves on their ability to detect when an animal is stressed ... A slow, tactical withdrawal usually avoids any danger.

Filming small creatures is not usually fraught with danger, but macrophotographer Stephen Bolwell once had a nasty experience when filming insects, spiders and scorpions in the Serengeti. The crew had only one vehicle and they wanted to go off in search of bigger game:

'Because I was filming the smaller things they used to just dump me and drive off. Normally you don't walk round there. It's not like the New Forest. But they just left me, and while I was there I saw the whole world go by – I was attacked by baboons – that was interesting. The big males were charging at me, coming to within about five or six feet. So I behaved in a non-threatening way. I thought this was the best move. Then a buffalo – one of the most dangerous animals in Africa – charged me. They don't just charge you; they stomp all over you and pulp you into the ground.'

On another occasion Stephen was assisting cameraman Hugh Maynard in East Africa and they were trying to scare a kestrel into the open:

'I wandered in amongst some rocks to see where this kestrel had landed.

'"Can you see it?"' Hugh shouted.

'"Yes," I called back.

'"So just walk a bit nearer and I'll get a shot as it flies out."

'I did what I needed to do and Hugh got his shot. Then I came bounding out, and he said, "What's the problem?"

'I said, "I just walked straight into a lion! He was as startled to see me as I was to see him."

'Hugh said nothing much about it and we got into the Landrover and drove off. Just then, Hugh saw the lion and said, "There's a lion there."

'I said, "Yes, I told you."

'He said, "I didn't believe you. You weren't running fast enough!"'

Veteran filmmaker Alan Root has been in a few scrapes and he would be the first to admit that a lot of the danger is of his own making:

'Most work is done from inside a vehicle, certainly if you're studying a dangerous species. You watch it from the safety of your Landrover. Even so, it can be dangerous. I had an accident a while ago that was purely my own fault. I was walking around on a rocky hill and came to the edge of a ledge. I looked down and there was a dead jackal below. I should have thought about it a bit longer, but I decided to jump down and take a closer look. I didn't realize that I was standing on an overhang and the leopard that had just killed the jackal was crouched immediately below me. So I jumped down and landed with my knees bent and my backside sticking out, right in this thing's face. It promptly savaged my left buttock and then ran away. It left me shaken but not badly hurt. Lots of blood was pouring down my leg, so we drove back to the warden's office. Myles Turner [the warden], who was an old friend, was there, and I limped into his office and said, "One of your leopards has bitten me on the bum," and he gave me this very cool look and said, "You know you're not allowed to feed the animals in the park!"'

On another occasion, Alan and Barry Paine were returning to base in Alan's Landrover when they ran out of petrol. They got out, surveyed the scene and were just about to set off with an empty can to find fuel when Alan remembered that he had a reserve tank with sufficient fuel to get them home. Driving up the track to a ridge overlooking the place where they had stopped, they came across a large pride of lions that had clearly been watching them. Alan turned to Barry and said, 'Now that would have been an interesting stroll!'

Even the most innocuous of creatures can be unpleasant when they want to be.

The late filmmaker Joan Root with an assortment of neighbours.

Producer Peter Bassett was working on *Life in the Undergrowth* when he went into anaphylactic shock from an allergic reaction to caterpillar hairs; when filming for *The Life of Birds* he had a bunch of angry fieldfares defend their nest site by defecating on him. Only his glasses saved him from one in the eye. While filming a flock of red-billed quelea –the largest flock of birds ever to have been caught on camera – the *Planet Earth* crew were covered with bird droppings, and with a flock of that size the unpleasantness was magnified greatly: both camera and cameraman were covered from top to toe. And almost everybody who has been anywhere near a tern or gull colony or a skua nest has been dive-bombed mercilessly by birds defending their nest site.

Bloodsuckers

The number one danger in the tropics, however, is not a large and menacing carnivore or an aerobatic bird, but a tiny bloodsucker – the mosquito. More deaths have been attributed to this little creature than to the total number of attacks by all the large predators combined. By the Rio Xingu in the Brazilian Amazon, according to *Andes to Amazon* producer Huw Cordey, all work stopped at 18.25 precisely. All the cooking, washing up and other chores were completed and everybody repaired to their tents and mosquito nets, for at 18.30 precisely every female mosquito in the area was on the wing and searching for her evening meal of blood. On another assignment Steve Nichols met mosquitoes while trying to film crocodiles hatching at night in Florida Bay, reputed to be the worst place in the world for the little blighters.

'We simply couldn't breathe. Once you put battery lights on, which attracted all

One of the more friendly occurences on Ândes to Amazon *– huge swarms of butterflies suck up water from the damp sand in Peru in order to get minerals and replace salts.*

sorts of other insects as well, you had to wear a handkerchief over your mouth to prevent yourself from choking on mosquitoes. The cameraman was up to his waist in water, filming the baby crocodiles as they swam off into the mangroves, and I was next to him hanging on to the light. We filmed for about three-quarters of an hour and I had been bitten on just about every available place, and then I suffered a complete allergic shock reaction. My vision went black and white, the cameraman's voice receded into the distance and all I can remember for about 20 minutes is this vague voice shouting, "Will you hold the light still!"'

Insects and insect-borne diseases are probably the greatest hazards facing wildlife filmmakers, and sometimes it's not only the film that is brought home; the wretched creatures come too. Robin Prytherch, then an assistant producer, remembers an occasion in the early 1970s when he was working with Jeffery Boswall and Doug Fisher on their expedition series *Wildlife Safari to the Argentine*. They were on the open mountainside of the high Alto Plano, looking for vicuñas:

'I remember I was in a vehicle one day and I felt this odd pain in my back. It was short-lived but painful enough to make me grasp my back and think, "Oh gosh, what was that?" Then it was all over and I forgot about it. Coincidentally, my hands became terribly burned from the sun. The air is thin up there and you burn easily, but I hadn't realized that while I was using the binoculars frequently the backs of my hands were burning. The result was gangrenous fingernails – quite nasty. So I went to the hospital and they took a look, and then I mentioned the pain in my back. They said I had a boil and that it would go away after a while. By the time I got to Buenos Aires at the end of the trip my hands were playing up, so I went to the British hospital. They took a look at my hands and scratched their heads, at which point I said, "By the way, I've got this thing on my back." They looked at it and said, "It's just a boil, it'll go away." Eventually I got home and had to see the BBC doctor for a check-up. By then my nails were beginning to heal. Several nails had dropped out and their replacements were growing – a bit grizzly – but then I said to the doctor, "By the way, I've got this thing on my back," and he said, "Oh, it's just a boil, it'll go away." A few weeks later, I went to see my own doctor and said, "Oh, by the way, I have this thing on my back" and by now it was

Insects and insect-borne diseases are probably the greatest hazards facing wildlife filmmakers, and sometimes it's not only the film that is brought home; the wretched creatures come too.

annoying me because it was weeping and uncomfortable. He gave me some antibiotics. Then I was at home one evening dressing this wound, when I felt a lump. I got hold of it and yanked it, and brought out an object about three-quarters of an inch long by a quarter of an inch in diameter … with moving parts! It was obviously a grub of some sort. I put it into a box and got into the office and phoned the doctor. "That thing on my back," I said, "was a grub." At first he said nothing and I said, "Are you still there?" He was completely dumbfounded, but then suggested I take it to the Bristol Health Clinic. They took a look and came back with a book, showing the relevant grubs. It turned out to be a botfly larva and they asked if they could keep it, as they didn't have a specimen.'

The last location tale is reserved for Keenan Smart, now head of the natural history unit at National Geographic, but once a rookie BBC producer. It was a baptism of fire – or rather blood. A roadside hotel served as his temporary home when he was due to film a bunch of vampire bats brought to him by one of the world's leading vampire-bat researchers.

'I was wondering how we were going to get these vampire bats into the hotel for the night. We also had a large bottle of blood for them that had to be refrigerated, so we had to sneak that in too. Dr Aurelio Malaga-Alba, the scientist with whom we were working, went to the front desk and I stood behind him holding the bat cage with a towel over it.

'He said, "I'd like a room for myself and my wife, and another for my friend here. We also have a vial of blood with us which we would like you to put in the hotel fridge." The receptionist asked, "Why do you have a vial of blood?" and Dr Malaga, as cool as a cucumber, looked him in the eye and said, "To feed my vampire bats, of course." At which point the receptionist burst out laughing, took the vial of blood and said no more.

'Dr Malaga then went to his room, opened the bathroom door and released the bats. He went to the hotel kitchen and came back with a saucer filled with blood. He put it on the bathroom floor and closed the door. The following morning I went in to collect the bats and I've never seen anything like it. It was like a scene from a Hitchcock film. It looked as if murder had been committed in this bathroom. Blood was everywhere – smeared on the walls, over the mirrors, on the floor – and hanging on the towel rail were seven very contented vampire bats!'

EMERGENCY

GIVEN THE REMOTE and often perilous places visited by wildlife film crews, the dangerous animals they encounter and the number of life-threatening diseases to which they are exposed, it is surprising that more people are not injured or taken seriously ill. Crews are trained in basic first aid and in how to survive in hostile environments, but there are times when things do get out of hand and it is often the little creatures that are the problem. While filming bonobos in the Congo, for instance, cameraman Martin Saunders was attacked by a swarm of bees. Just one sting is usually enough to strike a person down, but he was stung several times. Many miles from the nearest settlement, he went into anaphylactic shock, a worrying time for him and his producer. He survived and, as a consequence of that event, film crews routinely take adrenaline in their medical kit.

Cameraman Marin Saunders films mountain gorillas for Life on Earth.

All the precautions in the world, however, cannot make up for that 'dumb' moment. One crew went to film huge numbers of bats in caves in the USA. Local experts advised they wear protective clothing and breathe through respirators as the air in the caves was filled with the spores of a fungus that causes the respiratory disease histoplasmosis. Duly togged out, they entered the dark, dank interior and filmed the bats. After emerging, they carefully took off their protective clothing and rolled it up, but instead of packing it away in a bag and putting it in the boot of their car, they placed the contaminated overalls on the back seat. Later, both cameraman and producer went down with histoplasmosis. They, too, recovered, but it is a mistake they won't make again!

[CHAPTER SEVEN]

Playing with Time

During the hundred years since Oliver Pike made his groundbreaking films, the techniques for not only capturing images but also for manipulating them have developed to a staggering extent. Telephoto lenses enable a camera to be 500 metres (1600 feet) away from its subject, and macrolenses allow us to see insects as gigantic monsters. Time-lapse devices speed up time, so that plants seem to move like animals, and ultra-high-speed filming enables us to slow down and appreciate events that are over in the blink of an eye. This ability to readjust 'reality' so that we can see things that would otherwise be unseen is not a new development; it was challenging the earliest filmmakers at the beginning of the twentieth century. ☞

Above: Gerald Thompson was one of the first to research close-up filming: macrophotography.

Urban and His Protégés

Charles Urban (1867–1942) made a pioneering film about the ascent of Mont Blanc in 1902, and in 1903 he helped to kick-start the nature film business by employing Francis Martin Duncan (1873–1961). Like Muybridge, Duncan had begun by experimenting with sequence photography, but was soon to embrace moving pictures, especially microphotography. Together with Urban, he made several films that were played at the Alhambra Theatre in London as a quasi-scientific series called *The Unseen World*. Titles included *Rotifers*, *Water Flea* and *Octopus*, but the film that caught the public's imagination was *Cheese Mites* (1903). It started by showing a man looking at a piece of Stilton through a magnifying glass and then flinging his meal away, having seen what was crawling on it. The big close-ups had an impact in more ways that one: the cheese industry was in uproar.

Another of Urban's protégés was London-born Frank Percy Smith (1880–1945). Interested in exploring the educational value of moving wildlife pictures, he was employed at first by the Board of Education, but found that opportunities there were few. Nevertheless, he pioneered the use of the studio as a laboratory to become not only a leading scientific filmmaker but also one with the popular touch. He once described feeding his audience 'the powder of instruction in the jam of entertainment'.

Smith had caught Urban's eye with a still photograph showing a bluebottle's tongue, and was invited by the older man to repeat the exercise with moving pictures. With Urban's money and Smith's skill the two produced *The Balancing Bluebottle* (1908), which showed some quite extraordinary shots of a tethered fly juggling objects such as a cork, twigs or shells with its feet. Although more of a circus than an educational film, it did show the remarkable strength insects have compared to human beings, and attracted considerable positive press coverage. In 1911, Smith produced a similar film, *The Strength and Agility of Insects* (reissued in 1918 as *Nature's Acrobats*), with insects 'juggling' miniature dumbbells to show that they could carry objects many times their size and weight.

With Urban's money and Smith's skill the two produced The Balancing Bluebottle *(1908), which showed some quite extraordinary shots of a tethered fly juggling objects such as a cork, twigs or shells with its feet.*

Such was Smith's attention to detail that he would take up to two years to complete a film, inventing all manner of ways in which to capture the infinitesimally small or the slow – what was later to be called macro- and microphotography – or to speed up time using time-lapse techniques. At one stage he had alarms all over his house to wake him in the middle of the night so that he could adjust the camera or change the film. In 1910, he produced the masterpiece *Birth of a Flower*, the first major time-lapse film of plant growth and one distributed to this day.

During World War I, Smith became a photographer for the Royal Navy, while Urban produced war films. When hostilities ceased, Urban continued to walk the fine line between entertainment and science. In 1921, in collaboration with American zoologist and popularizer Raymond T. Ditmars, he produced *The Four Seasons*, which showed nature throughout the year. A frog, a beaver and a deer were the 'star performers', as the press called them, and, as one critic noted, the film boasted 'a cast more varied and temperamental than a Griffith play, a mise en scène more elaborate and spectacular than any setting ever devised by Von Stroheim or De Mille'. The combination of strong story and attractive images presented in an entertaining way is thought by some commentators to be the precursor of the television films that followed many years later.

Percy Smith, meanwhile, had gone back to working with Urban for a short time and then moved on to join British Instructional Films. By 1922, he had teamed up with Mary Field (who had worked with him on *Birth of a Flower*) and H. Bruce Woolfe to launch the series *Secrets of Nature*, whose first film was Oliver Pike's *The Cuckoo's Secret*, as we saw in Chapter One. Renamed *Secrets of Life* in 1933, it easily absorbed technological changes such as the coming of sound and the use of commentaries instead of captions, and ran successfully right up until the time of Smith's death in 1945.

While Smith was working in his studio in north London, another prolific filmmaker, James Williamson (1855–1933), was experimenting in Brighton. Born in Scotland, he had moved south and ran a chemist shop and photographic business in Hove. After making more than 128 short films in and around Brighton for his Kinematograph Company, he turned to wildlife. In *The History of a Butterfly: Romance of Insect Life* (1910), he filmed a captive female moth attracting males, butterfly caterpillars hatching from eggs, feeding and pupating, and finally the emergence of adult peacock and swallowtail butterflies.

Light, Science, Action

For the next big development in specialized wildlife filmmaking, we need to jump to the 1960s. While presenting the series *Look* (see Chapter Two), Peter Scott was approached by a scientist who had a series of still photographs showing the alder-wood wasp and its parasites. The pictures caught Scott's imagination and he was intrigued by the notion of parasites on parasites, which he thought would make an interesting edition of *Look*. There was only one drawback – no film. So he suggested to the scientist that he might consider filming the wasp. The scientist was somewhat taken aback: the technology needed to film such intimate detail had yet to be invented. To put it into the words of the scientist, 'It was one thing to suggest that one went away and made a film about the alder-wood wasp, but I don't think Sir Peter realized there were no standard techniques for filming insects ranging in size from an eighth-of-an-inch to three-quarters-of-an-inch, and filming their eggs, which of course, are minute.'

The scientist, though, was no ordinary scientist. He was Gerald Thompson (1917–2002), who went on to establish the specialist natural history filmmaking company Oxford Scientific Films. Back then, however, he and assistant Eric Skinner had some research to do, not on wasps, but on very close-up filming – macrophotography.

One of the first problems was light. In order to shoot in colour, they had to pour an enormous amount of light on to the subject. It is a problem filmmakers have to this day, but in those pioneering days it was critical. Films of insects had been made before, but when the pictures showed, say, caterpillars writhing, it may have looked dramatic to the audience, but to the naturalist it indicated that the film's little stars were in their death throes. The filmmakers also had to magnify things up to ten times, and magnifying the picture meant magnifying any vibrations. Eventually, Wood and Skinner solved all these problems with a specially built macrophotography rig with lights shining through flasks of water in order to keep their subjects cool. And this is how they came to film the alder-wood wasp, a film that went on to win a nature film competition organized by the BBC and the Council of Nature, assuring it an airing on *Look* in 1960. The audience was as captivated as Peter Scott had been, and the wasps marked another milestone in the history of wildlife filmmaking, a glimmer of a new era of television in which filmmakers would start to push back the frontiers of science to find new ways of not only knowing but also showing this hidden world.

One series that certainly pushed the boundaries was David Attenborough's *The Private Life of Plants* (1995). Until then, time-lapse had been something of a gimmick, but the production team on this series turned it into an art form. Time-lapse photography is a way of apparently speeding up time. The camera is triggered to take a single frame of a subject at regular intervals, the film travelling through the camera not at the conventional 25 (UK) or 24 (US) frames per second, but maybe one frame every minute or every hour. Playing it back at normal speed 'speeds up' the action, so that something that might take days or weeks, such as flowers opening or plants spreading across a meadow, can be condensed into a few seconds.

Until *The Private Life of Plants*, time-lapse had been recorded with a camera anchored to the spot – 'locked off' on a particular scene, plant or animal. It did not move. This meant that the time-lapse scene was more of a portrait than an action shot. In this production, though, the time-lapse camera moved, a new technique called 'tracking time-lapse'. For producer Neil Lucas, cameraman Tim Shepherd and camera boffin Martin Schann, it meant going back to the drawing board, literally, to design and develop the system. It was cutting-edge stuff, with Neil often stopping by Martin's workshop to pick up the latest version of the rig on his way to Heathrow and a foreign filming trip. In the field, slide rules, set squares and graph paper appeared as often as close-up lenses. The result was a series of extraordinary pictures of developing plants, in which the camera moves alongside the plant as it grows.

The same group of filmmakers developed a radically new system for capturing time-lapse images. It relies not on individual still frames from a film camera but on a digital stills camera. A special computer program joins the frames together to give a moving picture of the highest quality, even more detailed than high definition. This technique was used to great effect in a sequence in *Planet Earth* in which fungal parasites were shown invading an ant's head; cameraman Peter Kragh also took it under water to give a new perspective on corals feeding.

In the Flick of a Salamander's Tongue

A related technique is called not time-lapse but 'lapsed time'. The principle is the same but lapsed time is used to record events over an even longer period, such as the changing seasons. Leaving a time-lapse camera out in all weathers is impractical, so a camera is placed on a 'time post', film is shot of the scene and then the camera is removed. Some time later, the camera is placed in exactly the same position on the same time post and more film is taken. The pictures from each session can then be blended together to give a feeling of the passage of time. Lapsed time is used, for example, to show how the leaves on trees vary in quantity and colour through the seasons or to illustrate the sequence of wild flowers on the woodland floor in spring. This was done to great effect in *Living Britain* in 1999 and again in *Nature of Britain* in 2007. In the jungle episode of *Planet Earth,* cameras on time posts took one frame a week for four years to show the regeneration of rainforest in Borneo.

At the other end of the time spectrum is slow motion. In this case, the camera is 'over-cranked', meaning that the film is fed through the gate faster than usual, so when it is played back it slows down very fast action. Most film of birds in flight is slowed down slightly, so that they appear more majestic than frantic – very high-speed

cinematography can slow down a hummingbird's wings so that every twist and turn that keeps the bird in the air can be analysed.

High-speed film cameras whizz through a roll of film in seconds, and operators can never be sure that they have caught the action: it is very much a hit-or-miss affair. Today, digital technology has taken over. A high-speed digital camera can operate at a speed in excess of a thousand frames per second and the camera operator can be sure there and then that they have the shot. The digital camera is recording continuously on its hard drive, so when the operator presses the trigger the camera has already recorded the previous few seconds. The risk of missing something because of any delay in the operator's response is thus eliminated and the entire event can be downloaded intact on to a hard disk, DVD or video-tape. A most extraordinary image was obtained in 2004 when the *Animal Camera* team was testing one of these cameras. They placed a balloon filled with water over presenter Steve Leonard's head and popped it with a pin. The fabric of the balloon shrank in an instant, leaving the water 'hanging' in midair, before dropping slowly like treacle. In the series, this technique was used to capture the fastest movements in nature, contenders being the flick of a salamander's tongue, the karate chop of a mantis shrimp and the trap-jaw ant snapping its mandibles shut in less than the blink of an eye.

In the jungle episode of Planet Earth, *cameras on time posts took one frame a week for four years to show the regeneration of rainforest in Borneo.*

The most awesome shots using the ultra-high-speed video camera, though, must be those obtained by Simon King of the moment a great white shark leaps clear of the water in pursuit of its prey. The sequence was shown in *Planet Earth* and it led to one American viewer writing that he thought it 'the most amazing thing in a show of amazing things'.

You Can't Put a Camera There

Some optical devices are borrowed from other professions and adapted to suit the filmmakers' purposes. David Attenborough remembers wanting to film the Australian platypus in its nest burrow at the time of *Life on Earth* and being told it could not be

David Attenborough said of his encounter with a Rafflesia flower, 'Finding a flower with such a brief life is clearly not easy ... a never-to-be-forgotten thrill.'

done. By the time he returned to the subject in *The Life of Mammals* 25 years later the technology was available – thanks to developments in the medical world. Platypus researcher Tanya Rankin radio-tagged a platypus and plotted where its long tunnel ended in a nest chamber. Cameraman Mark Lambaugh was then able to push an endoscope down through the earth and into the burrow and get the shot, the first time ever.

The endoscope is a flexible tube with its own light source that is more usually used to inspect the internal organs or in minimally invasive surgery, but it can enable the filmmaker to get into places that would otherwise be impossible to reach, such as the insides of burrows or the nests of social insects. A variation on this is a probe with a miniature camera and lens at its movable tip that was developed to allow engineers to inspect the insides of aircraft. This too has been used to enter those hard-to-get-at places, such as the inside of a driver ant's nest in Kenya for *Natural World: Ant Attack* in 2006.

Another close-up lens is the straightscope or borescope, used for deep-focus macroshots. In this case, the subject in the foreground, such as an insect, can be big in frame but the background also remains in focus, a bonus when the depth of field would normally be limited. Variations on this include the 90-degree periscope and the 45-degree prism system, which enable the cameraman to look round corners.

New devices are being developed daily and these specialist filming techniques have taken filmmakers in some bizarre directions. Independent producer John Downer

Filming hummingbirds feeding for Life of Birds.

has explored many of them: he has had cameras hidden inside a model truck dressed as a small furry mammal in *The Making of Supersense* (1989), in an artificial stone as 'bouldercam' in *Lions: Spy in the Den* (2000) and in elephant dung as 'dungcam' for *Elephants: Spy in the Herd* (2003). All of these and more, an armoury of upwards of 20 hidden cameras, including 'tortoisecam', 'croccam', 'hippocam', 'dragonflycam' and 'stealthcam', were assembled for *Trek: Spy on the Wildebeest* (2007).

One of John's pioneering films was *Wildlife on One: In-flight Movie* (1987), in which new filming techniques brought to life the experience of flying like a bird. Camera tucked under his arm, John was winched up and kept aloft by a parachute being towed behind a car while he 'flew' alongside a trained duck. The technique was to be used in many bird films that followed.

Bring in the Birds

While most of *The Life of Birds* showed wild birds behaving naturally – the result of good fieldcraft on the part of those making the series – some sequences needed a bit of help. To enable the crew to take close-ups of ducks in flight, some birds were imprinted on one of the consultants, Conrad Maufe. He became the 'duck mother' and the birds would follow him everywhere. In one sequence, Conrad drove along the edge of a Welsh reservoir and cameraman Mike Potts sat beside him filming the bird flying a few metres away. The bird, a drake, flew past David Attenborough delivering a piece to camera and then settled on the water next to a gaggle of females. It had returned successfully to the wild, the lure of the opposite sex stronger than the bond with its surrogate mother.

Trained birds were needed in an episode of *Predators* in 2000, when the team wanted

Top: An elephant uses its foot to explore dungcam, a remote-controlled camera used for filming Elephants: Spy in the Herd.

Above: John Downer filming imprinted teal from a parascender for Supersense.

close-up shots of a great grey owl hunting. Film of hunting in the wild was in the can, but some big close-ups of the final moment of capture would give the sequence more impact. So off they went to the Birds of Prey Centre, where a couple of owls had been taught to fly to a buzzer buried in some artificial snow. Gavin Maxwell directed the first shoot, but his bird flew into a tree and resolutely refused to come down. A week later producer Peter Bassett and researcher Amanda Kear tried again with bird number two, a younger one.

'That one was waaaaaay too smart for its own good,' Amanda recalls. 'After a couple of flights to the buzzer, it quickly figured out what human beings pointing meant. So it flew to anything someone pointed at, anticipating that the buzzer was buried there and would buzz in a minute or two. It became ludicrous when I said, "That's your tea over there, Pete" and it flew down to perch on his mug. In the end, when setting up the next shots the team had to block the owl's view and be very careful not to point!'

Trained or imprinted birds have long been used to get close-up shots of eagles, owls and swans. The magnificent golden eagle at the start of *The Living Isles* and

Opposite: Alan Hayward filming imprinted pigeon for In-Flight Movie.

Left: Greylag geese are imprinted to follow a microlite during the filming of Supernatural.

Wildlife Special: Eagle which lands so perfectly on a rock directly in front of the camera; the whooper swans following Alan Titchmarsh's speedboat in *British Isles: A Natural History* and the champion peregrine in the hot-air balloon in *Steve Leonard's Ultimate Killers* were courtesy of such skilled bird handlers as Lloyd Buck, but for sheer spectacle nothing, perhaps, can beat the sight of a flock of sandhill cranes following the ultralight of ornithologist Dan Sprague in *Natural World: Flying Home*.

To get up there with the birds, wildlife camera folk have purloined all manner of craft – aircraft, helicopters, balloons and dirigibles – used either as camera platforms or as means by which to survey large areas for widely spaced animals or choice locations. Des and Jen Bartlett spent hours flying over the Namib Desert in ultralights in search of desert elephants, the world's tallest, for *Survivors of the Skeleton Coast.* Werner Hertzog and Graham Dorrington floated over the canopy in Guyana rainforest in a miniature two-man airship for the feature *The White Diamond,* and cameraman Warwick Sloss and his French pilot flew gingerly around baobab trees in a precarious two-man hot-air balloon, known as a cinebule, for *Planet Earth.* The cinebule, especially, is not for the faint-hearted. The pilot

Imprinted whooper swans follow their human 'parents' during the filming of Journey of Life.

managed to collide with the trees they were filming and get wrapped up in the branches on more than one occasion. Warwick survived intact, but is unlikely to return to that kind of camera platform in a hurry.

Helicopters have come into their own since the invention of camera and lens mounts that are steadied by gyroscopes, enabling filmmakers to zoom in from very wide shots of a landscape to big close-ups of animals or people below, and vice versa, while the helicopter hovers quite high in the sky. Until this development, helicopters tended to disturb animals. Many early aerials from East Africa show animals racing for their lives and this was deemed unethical, so helicopters and fixed-wing aircraft came to be used mainly for aerial scenics. The camera was mounted either on the side of the machine or under the nose, with little flexibility of movement, mainly tilting up and down.

Dolly on the Rails

More flexibility and greater precision is now achieved using new gyroscopically steadied camera systems like the Heligimbal (see page 135). Model helicopters carrying lightweight cameras are used where the big ones cannot go. The shot in which the camera rises above David Attenborough and the magnificent statues of Easter Island at the end of *State of the Planet* was achieved with a model helicopter and the expertise of miniature-camera specialist Geoff Bell.

Flying through the woodland canopy, say, can also be achieved with a 'cable dolly'. In this case, a wire is strung between two trees and a dolly or mobile camera platform with a camera is hung from it. The camera can then be pulled or pushed along the cable, giving the cameraman the ability to 'fly' the camera through the forest without the need for an expensive rail-and-dolly rig.

A dolly on rails, however, comes into its own when a moving shot has to be repeated over and over again with the camera in exactly the same place. This kind of device is called a motion-control rig, and computers control the latest ones. In the making of *Perfect Shark,* the rig was used to film presenter Mike de Gruy in a 'virtual' studio – a studio with a black background and nothing else. The co-ordinates of the moves to be made by the camera were plotted on the computer by Red Vision designers Peter Bailey and Sue Land and fed into the rig's memory. The rig then duplicated those shots in the studio, without anybody having to touch the camera. After the studio session was complete, the actual scene – a virtual aquarium through which Mike was seen to walk – replaced the black background. He could also be seen interacting with fossil sharks that 'came to life'. In reality, he had to react to something that was not there, for the sharks were also the product of the computer.

Seeing something that is not there applies to night filming, too. In the early days, night scenes were shot with bright lights, but filmmakers were quick to realize that this affected the behaviour of animals and in some cases compromised their very survival. Today, there are more acceptable methods of seeing in the dark. The simplest is the use of infrared lights to illuminate the scene. In the main (rattlesnakes and boas excepted), animals do not detect infrared, so the lights do not affect their behaviour. The only drawback is that the pictures come out in black and white. Camerawoman Justine Evans, however, was able to use infrared lights effectively when filming David Attenborough with oilbirds in a cave in Venezuela for *The Life of Birds* and to capture the harrowing images of one of Africa's largest pride of lions attacking elephants at night in *Planet Earth*.

Miniature infrared lights and cameras were employed to film the behaviour of baboons at night in *Animal Camera*. Producer Andrew Murray and his crew squeezed through the manhole-sized entrance to the baboons' cave during the day in order to rig the camera system and then left before the animals returned in the evening. The baboons were able to carry on their business unaware that they were being filmed. The resulting sequence showed how baboons use special grunts to find family members in the dark.

An alternative is the 'starlight camera', developed by the military and for security systems, which operates just as it says – in little more than starlight. It was used to film what is probably the shyest bird in the world – the kiwi – for another episode in *The Life of Birds*. Series producer Mike Salisbury went to New Zealand and found that, despite being the country's national symbol, this nocturnal bird was not easy to track down. The experts failed to come up trumps, but Mike was fortunate to meet a man in a bar in Invercargill, at the southernmost tip of the South Island, who said kiwis could be found even further south, on Stewart Island. Mike headed out there and touched base with a local naturalist who knew exactly where to look. Mike was taken in a small boat around a headland to a secluded bay and crouched down on the sand just as two birds came along the shoreline, feeding on sandhoppers. He returned a year later with David Attenborough and they were able to capture the perfect sequence, courtesy of the starlight camera.

The specially-constructed antcam used in Tanzania to film driver ants for Killer Ants, *an episode of the* Natural World.

Sit Back and Let the Creatures Do the Work

Perhaps the most extraordinary wildlife filming technique is the onboard camera. Getting animals to film themselves, without human intervention, has always been a dream, but in 1993 the production team of BBC1's *Wildlife Special: Great White Shark* joined forces with National Geographic's Greg Marshall and attached an onboard camera, dubbed 'crittercam', to a great white shark. Greg had been developing the system since 1986 and has since attached it to whales, seals, penguins, turtles, other sharks and a sturgeon. Its first trial was with a loggerhead turtle, to test whether it interfered with the animal's everyday life. When the turtle dived and surfaced without problems, the device was judged ready to be tried on other marine animals, including one of the ocean's most formidable predators.

First, a shark was attracted to the boat by putting out a slick of mashed-up fish – the chum – and, once it was alongside, a small dart, similar to those used in shark-tracking studies but with the crittercam attached, was pushed into its back. The device consisted of a torpedo-shaped body containing the camera, with fins on either side that ensured it remained the right way up. It trailed alongside the shark's dorsal fin, giving a shark's-eye view. In due course a special link between crittercam and shark dissolved in the sea water, releasing the camera to float to the surface some time later. An inbuilt 'pinger' enabled the crew to find and recover it. The pictures from this particular excursion showed how the shark dived to the bottom and stalked its prey from below – behaviour that had been theorized but was now established as fact.

> *Today, there are more acceptable methods of seeing in the dark. The simplest is the use of infrared lights to illuminate the scene. In the main (rattlesnakes and boas excepted), animals do not detect infrared, so the lights do not affect their behaviour.*

Subsequent versions of the crittercam have been less invasive. Suction cups, fin clamps and adhesive mounts have replaced the dart, and the device itself is much smaller and shaped to minimize drag. It has proved popular with scientists and filmmakers alike. For the scientist, it can log such information as depth, pressure, temperature and time, and for the filmmaker there is the animal's-eye view of its natural environment. The ultimate crittercam shot, of course, will be that elusive sperm whale and giant squid encounter, but they still have to work out a way to get light down there in the deep.

Terrestrial crittercam has not been far behind, with cameras on bears, lions, hyenas and domestic dogs and cats, the difference being that signals can be obtained directly from the camera and it can be switched on and off at will, thus preserving battery power. In Peter Bassett's *Lion Battlefield* a serval hunting birds on the ground was equipped with a miniature camera and the resulting pictures revealed something else that was new to science. During filming, shadows and the direction of the sun caught Pete's eye. When the serval was not hunting, it walked in any direction, but when it started to stalk its shadow was always in front. It hunted with the sun behind it, so that any prey that glanced up would be looking directly into the sun and be less likely to see it approaching.

A golden eagle is fitted with a specially adapted lightweight video camera for Wildlife Special: Eagle.

The terrestrial units can be tiny and this is precisely what Pete and his team explored in *Animal Camera*. Using technology that is more often applied to mobile phones, onboard camera guru Jonathan Watts designed and built a new style of device that was light enough to be carried aloft by a bird and not interfere with its flight. A golden eagle was the first to test it, and the speed with which the bird dropped down on to prey or the way it barrel-rolled when buzzed by a buzzard was breathtaking, but the real revelation came when a camera was placed on a racing pigeon. On the journey back to its home loft, the bird did not travel 'as the crow flies', but followed roads and railways all the way. In the same series, a bumblebee wearing a tracking device could be followed everywhere it went. With miniature cameras getting smaller and smaller, there may come a time when fly-on-the-wall documentaries are actually filmed by the fly on the wall.

HELICOPTERS AND HELIGIMBALS

HELICOPTERS HAVE OFTEN been used both for transport and as camera platforms, but they really came into their own with the introduction of new camera mounts like the Cineflex Heligimbal, which separates the camera, such as the Sony HDC-950, from the powerful 400mm Canon HJ40 lens, so that the lens is outside and the camera and monitor inside. Using this system, the helicopter can be as much as 1 kilometer (over half a mile) away from the subject and therefore less likely to disturb it. A gyroscopic damping system ensures the image is rock steady even though the helicopter itself is shaking.

This technology was used to good effect in *Planet Earth* (2006), when animals such as wild dogs or wolves were tracked in their natural habitats from hundreds of metres away, giving a new perspective on familiar behaviour. In Bahrain, the bleak isolation of seabirds nesting on the edge of the desert could be seen clearly from the air. In the Canadian Arctic, with the sea ice unreliable and difficult if not impossible to walk on, the production team had helicopters to get them close to polar bears. In order not to disturb them, they hovered very high up and used the very long lens. Similarly, the team covering the end of the snow goose migration had to be airlifted into an area of remote tundra. They camped in the icy cold for four weeks, but it was all worth it. From a helicopter, they filmed a vast flock of geese estimated to be 20 kilometres (12 miles) long and 5 kilometres (3 miles) wide, an extraordinary natural spectacle that had never been filmed before.

A photograph of Iguazu Falls on the Brazil–Argentina border by aerial photographer Robert Fulton.

[CHAPTER EIGHT]

Under the Sea

If you asked most people to name the first person to film under water, they would probably say the Frenchman Jacques-Yves Cousteau. If the same question were put to diving enthusiasts or viewers of a certain age, they might suggest Austrian husband-and-wife team Hans and Lotte Hass. Certainly Cousteau and the Hasses were among the first to swim freely under water with cameras some 50 years ago, but the very first exponent was actually an American, J. Ernest Williamson (1881–1966). ☞

Above: Peter Scoones filming captive bluefin tuna in Japan for Blue Planet.

Many Leagues

It all started with Williamson's father, Charles Williamson, of Norfolk, Virginia. He had invented a device, consisting of a tube with a series of interlocking, concentric rings, that when suspended from a suitably equipped ship could pump down air and retain communication with a diver 80 metres (250 feet) below the surface of the sea.

Williamson Junior's device was primarily designed for salvage work and ship repairs, but then a journalist, he realized it could also be used to help take photographs under water and in 1912 he designed a special vessel for the purpose. It consisted of a metal sphere (like the bathysphere invented many years later) in which the camera operator sat, with a funnel-shaped compartment on the side to hold the camera. The funnel was fronted with a 1.5-metre (5-foot) diameter observation window, 4 cm (1½ inches) thick. Williamson called his invention the Williamson Photosphere and its first trial was off the coast of Virginia, at the bottom of Chesapeake Bay. From the mother ship, a large light was hung so that it shone just in front of the tube, enabling Williamson to photograph anything that swam past the window. The experiment was such a success that he was persuaded to use the same technique to obtain moving pictures under water.

Ernest and his brother George – the embryonic Submarine Film Corporation – took the photosphere to the crystal-clear waters of the Bahamas, where light filters down to depths in excess of 45 metres (150 feet). Here, in March 1914, Ernest shot the very first underwater motion pictures. His first film was *Thirty Leagues Under the Sea* and in August it premiered at the American Museum of Natural History in New York. The film's climax shows Ernest wrestling with and then killing a shark with a knife right in front of the photosphere's observation window.

By the spring of 1916, the photosphere was being used to film scenes for a Universal Pictures feature based on Jules Verne's *Twenty Thousand Leagues Under the Sea*. It was not easy. Any significant swell rocked the barge and photosphere uncontrollably and any storm clouded the water with sediment so that nothing could be seen. Shoals of inquisitive barracudas harassed men in diving suits who were playing the parts of Captain Nemo's crew. Nevertheless, the film

> *In March 1914, Ernest Williamson shot the very first underwater motion pictures. His first film was* Thirty Leagues Under the Sea *and in August it premiered at the American Museum of Natural History in New York.*

was completed and both documentary and feature attracted large and enthusiastic audiences in New York, Chicago and London. Decades later, Williamson was asked to advise on Disney's 1954 remake of *Twenty Thousand Leagues Under the Sea* and significantly the film crew opted for the same locations that he had used 38 years before.

By 1932, a compilation of previous films with the title *Williamson Beneath the Sea* showed how the photosphere was used not only as a filming platform but as an observation chamber from which museum scientists at both the American Museum of Natural History and the Field Museum in Chicago could gain first-hand observations that helped them construct their coral-reef dioramas. In 1939, the Bahamas–Williamson Expedition involved filming from the photosphere for scientific purposes and introduced the viewing audience to Williamson's wife and daughter, the latter known affectionately as 'the little captain'. The photosphere also became a temporary underwater post office – the world's first – with an issue of Bahamas stamps that celebrated Williamson's underwater filming adventures.

For over 50 years, Williamson was responsible for the underwater scenes in many Hollywood movies, but rather than be lured by the ease of working in a 'tank' he always sought to take his pictures from his photosphere. His last film was a compilation of his previous work in a half-hour cut-down of *Williamson Beneath the Sea* for the television series *I Search for Adventure*. The year was 1955.

In the meantime, the Europeans were following a different path, adopting a more flexible approach to exploring the ocean. They were helped by a broad-bladed fin or flippers, designed in 1935 by the Frenchman Louis de Corlieu, and some form of self-contained breathing apparatus, a dream of Leonardo da Vinci in the sixteenth century but the reality of a succession of inventors that culminated in the 'aqualung' developed by Jacques-Yves Cousteau and Emile Gagnan in 1942–3.

Hass and the Frogmen

First to see this approach as a way to make underwater wildlife films was the Austrian Hans Hass. It seems rather curious that an underwater pioneer should hail from a landlocked nation, but Hass, his wife Lotte and the crew aboard their magnificent white sailing ship, the *Xarifa*, inspired an entire generation of swim-divers.

Hans started out hunting fish with Fernez goggles and a hand-held harpoon at Cap d'Antibes in the south of France in 1937 at the age of 18, but two years later, visiting Curaçao and Bonaire in the Dutch West Indies, he discovered that watching and filming fish was more interesting than killing them. It led to his first underwater film, *Stalking Beneath the Sea,* about life in a coral reef. More importantly, the

Hans Hass photographing underwater during the filming of Diving to Adventure.

underwater world of the tropics had whetted his appetite. He switched, much to his father's annoyance, from reading law to studying zoology and planned an ambitious expedition that would take him around the world. In 1941, while still in his early twenties, he started to write and lecture in order to fund his dream, but with World War II raging in Europe any thoughts of exotic locations had to take a back seat and he had to be content with an excursion to the Aegean Sea.

Hass was conscripted by the Nazi Wehrmacht to join its elite 'frogmen' team, the Kleinkampfverband, whose activities remain poorly documented to this day on account of a code of secrecy. In 1942, however, he realized his dream and bought a research ship, the *Seeteufel*, only to have it confiscated by the Russians in 1945. Undeterred by the loss of all his money, he went to Liechtenstein, set up the International Institute for Submarine Research and was eventually able to purchase his own research ship, the *Xarifa*. In 1953, he began to dive and film on the great coral reefs of the world, funded by photo assignments and the BBC.

Until 1942, Hass had used an open diving helmet fed by an air pump at the surface, but now he experimented with flippers and a self-contained breathing apparatus designed by the Dräger Company in Lübeck, Germany. The bag was intended to be positioned on the chest, but Hass redesigned it so that it could be placed on the back. It enabled him to move about more like a fish than a man and added a new dimension to his second film, *Man Amongst Sharks* (1947), shot on his first excursion to the Red Sea, where he was able to observe and film reef fish, sharks and manta rays with the minimum of disturbance. Hass was the first diver to shake off the shackles of being a 'walk-diver', with helmet and boots with lead soles, and adopt the 'swim-dive' approach, a milestone in underwater filming history.

His second trip to the Red Sea, this time with his wife Lotte Baierl, nearly proved a disaster, not because of anything that happened during diving, but because the Swiss company that processed his film destroyed some of the negative … along with their wedding photos. Fortunately, there was enough footage unharmed to make *Under the Red Sea* (1951), which won an international prize for best documentary at the Venice Film Festival.

Hass was the first diver to shake off the shackles of being a 'walk-diver', with helmet and boots with lead soles, and adopt the 'swim-dive' approach, a milestone in underwater filming history.

In 1953 and 1954, the Caribbean and Galapagos Islands were the locations for Hans and Lotte's *Diving to Adventure* series, followed in 1957–8 by the Red Sea and the Indian Ocean. *Undersea World of Adventure* followed in 1958 and *Adventure* during 1959 and 1960. By 1962, the Hasses had made over a hundred underwater films.

Sharks were frequently before the cameras, but for the first time they were being seen in a different light – not as the bloodthirsty killers they had once been thought to be, but as nature's top predators with a beauty all of their own. Initially, however, Hans Hass had difficulty convincing people of this. On a visit to Australia's Great Barrier Reef in December 1952 he met a doctor who specialized in shark bites and insisted on showing Hass his photo album – a series of gruesome bite pictures – in an attempt to stop him diving with such fearsome creatures. Hass was not to be put off and the following day dived off Green Island, where he encountered a 3.5-metre (12-foot) great hammerhead. The shark approached to within 1 metre (3 feet) and Hass was able to take the first ever picture of this great creature. Similarly, a historic first encounter with sperm whales showed these gentle giants to be shy of people, not at all the aggressive beasts depicted in Herman Melville's *Moby Dick*.

Captain Cousteau: Oceanographic Technician

Although Hans and Lotte were enormously influential, film and television's most celebrated underwater filmmaker is without doubt Jacques-Yves Cousteau. The son of a wealthy lawyer, born in the Gironde area of southwest France in 1910, he travelled frequently as a result of his father's work and had his first taste of diving in Lake Harvey, while on holiday in Vermont. His first professional contact with the sea was at the French naval academy in Brest. Ironically, the air rather than the sea was his first love. He joined the naval aviation school, but a near fatal car accident meant he could not acquire his wings. Denied the right to fly, he swam instead.

In 1943, while a lieutenant in the French navy, Cousteau helped develop the aqualung, a breathing device that was to revolutionize underwater swimming and make scuba diving a reality for millions of enthusiasts the world over. After the war, he helped found the French navy's Undersea Research Group and in 1950, through the patronage of a wealthy donor, the Direction Générale du Cinéma Français, the navy and the Ministry of Education, he was appointed commander of the research ship *Calypso*, a converted British minesweeper that was to be his home for long periods throughout the rest of his life. He made 30 voyages and a plethora of films, both for the cinema and television, obtaining the first colour film from the ocean's depths in the Red Sea in 1952.

His first major film, *The Silent World* (1956), gained him an Academy Award® for best documentary feature and the Palme d'Or at the Festival de Cannes. More honours followed, with Oscars® awarded to *The Golden Fish* (1959) and *The World Without Sun* (1964). His foray into television began in 1966 with *The World of Jacques-Yves Cousteau*, later *The Undersea World of Jacques-Yves Cousteau*, which

Jacques Cousteau diving underwater with custom camera.

Captain Jacques-Yves Cousteau and his famous red woollen cap.

played in BBC2's *The World About Us* strand from 1968 to 1976; then came *Oasis in Space*, the *Cousteau Odyssey* series, the *Cousteau Amazon* series and *Cousteau's Rediscovery of the World.*

Cousteau liked to call himself an 'oceanographic technician'. French president Jacques Chirac dubbed him an 'enchanter'. US president Bill Clinton described him as a man of 'rare insight and extraordinary spirit'. Universally, he was 'Captain Cousteau'.

He is probably remembered as much for his soft and unrelenting French accent and red woollen cap as for the stunning images taken by his talented underwater cameramen. In film and television terms, he was a showman and his method of communicating the marine sciences, a simple means of sharing complex concepts, was often criticized by academics, yet became the way of television generally. Jacques Cousteau reached millions of people all over the world and was actively campaigning for the environment right up to the time of his death in Paris in 1997.

Shark Summoning and the Real 'Jaws'

While the Hasses and Cousteau were kick-starting swim-diving, a small army of underwater photographers was following close behind, each a pioneer in his or her own right. One of the first was US blueberry farmer Stan Waterman, son of a wealthy cigar manufacturer. His first contact with diving came when he was given a pair of Ama pearl-diving goggles brought back from Japan by a family friend. The year was 1936 and Waterman was 13 years old, but the seed had been sown. In 1951, he purchased an aqualung set from a mail-order catalogue and dived for the first time in 4.5 metres (15 feet) of fresh water in Walkers Pond, Maine. His family looked on with some apprehension as he disappeared below the surface. He sat on a rock on the bottom of the pond, a moment that changed his life.

Waterman abandoned blueberries, commissioned the building of a boat – the *Zingaro* – gathered his family about him and headed for the Bahamas, where he started a diving business. Although he immediately acquired an underwater movie camera, filmmaking did not become the most important element in his life until 1965, when National Geographic bought rights in a family movie taken in Tahiti.

Then things took off.

In 1968, Waterman joined up with Peter Gimbel, Rodney Fox (one of the few to have been bitten seriously by a great white shark and survived) and Australians Ron and Valerie Taylor on an extraordinary adventure off the coast of South Africa. It resulted in the stunning feature film *Blue Water, White Death*. For the first time, divers were seen leaving their safety cages in the midst of a shark feeding frenzy. It was also the film that introduced us to 'white death' – the magnificent but infamous great white shark.

The great white was, of course, the principal villain in Peter Benchley's novel *Jaws*, which Stephen Spielberg turned into one of the scariest movies of all time. Ron and Valerie Taylor, working out of Adelaide, filmed the real-life shark sequences. They were the Antipodean answer to Hans and Lotte, except that Valerie wore a neon-pink wetsuit.

Stan Waterman, meanwhile, teamed up with Peter Benchley for ten years on ABC's *American Sportsman*, winning no fewer than five Emmies, the most collected by any underwater filmmaker. His first was with Benchley and his own son, Gordy

A great white shark is filmed from the safety of a shark cage off South Australia, the location for the real-like sharks in the feature film Jaws.

Waterman, swimming with manta rays at Marisula Seamount in the Sea of Cortez off the coast of Mexico.

Stan also co-directed, along with veteran underwater filmmaker Al Giddings, the underwater sequences for *The Deep* – another movie based on a Benchley novel – and introduced a budding cameraman to underwater films. This was Howard Hall, who was invited on to *The Deep* team to summon up sharks in the Coral Sea. With the money he earned, he had an underwater film camera built and tested it filming blue sharks off San Diego. One day when Stan asked Howard if he had any thoughts on a new film on sharks he had been commissioned to make for CBS, Howard mentioned that he had filmed blue sharks. On the strength of three rolls of film – the only three he had ever shot – he was invited to join the crew. The film was transmitted in the UK as part of the Survival Anglia strand on ITV.

Howard and the Bloodthirsty Squid

Howard Hall and his wife Michele went on to produce many award-winning films for television. *Seasons in the Sea* and *Shadows in a Desert Sea*, both made for PBS *Nature* and the BBC, were among them, the former winning a Golden Panda for 'Best of Festival' at Wildscreen 90 – the so-called 'green Oscars' held in Bristol, England every two years – and the latter 'Best Cinematography' at Wildscreen 92. Two years later a National Geographic Special *Jewels of the Caribbean Sea* picked up two Emmies.

Howard and his companions have had a number of amazing encounters with marine creatures, but none as bizarre as the night they first met giant Humboldt Current squid. They were diving at night in the Sea of Cortez. While angling over the side of the dive boat for bait to bring in the squid, Howard's father had snagged a thresher shark by the tail (more evidence, perhaps, that they stun their prey by thrashing it with their extremely long tail), and was about to release it for the cameramen in the water when Howard noticed flashing lights deep below him and heading rapidly towards the surface. A squid rushed past him and attached itself to the head of the shark. It was 1.5 metres (5 feet) long and on contact it flashed bright red to blinding white. Another squid shot past and caught a 1.2-metre (4-foot) long needlefish swimming at the surface. It seized the fish with two long tentacles and pulled it towards its grasping arms, tearing into the flesh with its parrot-like beak. Quite quickly the situation was out of control, with squid all over the place, jetting this way and that, catching fish put out as bait and literally tearing them apart.

Suddenly Howard was grabbed from behind, pulled downwards at least 3 metres (10 feet), then released. He approached a squid slicing into a skipjack tuna. Blood and scales clouded the water. He reached out to touch it. In a flash of colour, the squid grasped his hand and drew blood. Unlike octopuses and the more common squid, the Humboldt Current species have sharp hooks surrounding their sucker discs that dig into the flesh of their victims – these are serious predators.

The squid, however, were hard to film. They shunned the lights. One bonus, though, was that they did not harass the crew … except for one of the divers in the water. Alex Kerstitch was taking stills and had no movie lights around him. Without warning, three of these enormous beasts grabbed him by the scruff of the neck and dragged him down into the abyss. A tentacle wrapped around his neck and pulled off a gold medallion on a chain, cutting the skin on his neck. Another squid tore the diving computer from his pressure gauge and the third ripped his dive light from his wrist and the collecting bag from his waist; then, just as suddenly as they had appeared, they were gone. Alex had been mugged … by squid!

An Occupational Hazard

Danger comes with the job under water, but caution is the watchword and risks are carefully calculated. As Australian veteran Ben Cropp once said, 'There are bold divers and old divers, but there are no old, bold divers.' Ben himself had his hands full on one occasion when six bronze whalers – also known as copper sharks – were taking an unhealthy interest in him. He fended them off using his flippers, but kept on filming all the while.

Mike de Gruy and Paul Atkins dropped into the 'killing zone' when filming killer whales storming the seal and sea lion beaches in Patagonia for *Trials of Life*. The whales came right out of the water to snatch seals from the beach and flashed by within centimetres of the two divers. They were more intent on activity on the beach than in the water, so Mike and Paul, lying prone on the beach at the water's edge, were actually more at risk than they had been in the water, but fortunately they got their shots without coming to any harm.

The two took their lives into their hands on another occasion while filming tiger sharks in Hawaii. The sharks turn up at exactly the same time each year to patrol beaches where albatross fledglings are learning to fly. Any that ditch in the sea are shark fodder. At first, Mike and Paul filmed the sharks from the shore and from platforms over the sea, but they soon realized that the sharks were only interested in things at the surface. If they could swim below the sharks, the great beasts would ignore them. So they took a calculated risk and went free-diving with tiger sharks. Their hunch paid off and they were able to film events above and below the waves.

On a previous dive, however, Mike had nearly come a cropper to an aggressive grey reef shark in the South Pacific. He approached too closely, swimming into the shark's personal space. It savaged his arm, which still bears the scars.

While sharks are an obvious hazard in a tropical sea, those gentle giants humpback whales might seem like pussy cats in comparison. BBC producer Martha Holmes knows otherwise:

'Underwater cameraman Peter Scoones and I were trying to get shots of male humpback whales fighting, when I looked down and saw this huge humpback coming

Killer whales come right out of the sea to pluck sea lions from the beach during the making of Trials of Life.

out of the black and heading up towards us as fast it could go. I looked at Peter and we realized we only had a few seconds, so we swam out of the way fast. We moved so fast that people on the dive boat joked later that they thought we were walking on water. At the time, though, I thought this was curtains. His tail came within a metre of us. Had we been hit by that we would have been minced completely.'

Afterwards, Martha realized what had happened: the male humpback had spotted a rival. He had one thing on his mind – to see off the competition – and woe betide anything in his way.

On that occasion, the divers were in relatively clear waters, where they had no need to get too close to the action. In many cases, however, the cameraman must be close, because visibility under water is not what it is on land. The net result is that cameramen inevitably intimidate marine life – what Ben Cropp calls the 'underwater paparazzi' effect – and the subject either flees or fights. This is probably what happened when Australian 'crocodile hunter' and TV presenter Steve Irwin was killed in 2006. He swam over the top of a stingray – not the most sensible of places to be – and the ray, seeing a shadow above it, thought, 'Tiger shark' and struck out defensively.

Polecams, Towcams and Mighty Big Cams

One way to avoid confrontation is to use the new technology. A device known as a 'polecam' (basically a camera on a pole) can be placed over the side of a small boat

Cameraman Peter Scoones films a grey whale with a remote camera – a polecam – in the San Ignacio Lagoon, Baja California.

and the action followed on a television monitor. The sinister above-and-below-the-surface shots in *Wildlife Special: Great White Shark* were obtained in this way.

Another device is the 'towcam'. It consists of a camera in an underwater housing with stabilizing fins that can be towed behind a boat. An artificial lure attracts fast-swimming creatures in front of the lens. South African cameraman Charles Maxwell deployed his towcam for *Perfect Shark* and had tuna, mako and great white sharks chasing along behind the boat.

A free-swimming diver with a film or video camera in an underwater housing, however, carries out most underwater filming. The trend is for progressively smaller equipment, such as underwater digital video cameras, so imagine the problems of filming with a camera that takes at least three people to manhandle; this is the challenge of large-format cinematography under water.

The screen is big, the film is big, which means the camera is big ... very big, and therefore the dive boat must be big. Underwater filmmakers have described large-format camera systems as 'the most impractical motion-picture format for capturing underwater wildlife behaviour'. The basic camera weighs 115 kg (250 lb). Although neutrally buoyant when in the water, its very size means that normally gentle forces under the sea seem gargantuan. Simply holding position in a weak ocean current is difficult, so manoeuvring the camera upcurrent to a new location – usually child's play for an operator with the lightweight kit used for making television films – is almost impossible. Add to this an enormous tripod, the shearing effect of underwater surges (which can snap a tripod leg like a matchstick), an array of artificial lights, just three minutes of film in the magazine, a mechanism that sounds like a lawn mower, and a crew of half a dozen divers, and the chances of recording natural animal behaviour are limited. Many undersea creatures, especially sharks and whales, are very sensitive to sound and they do one of the few things the camera records regularly – they bolt. Howard Hall recalls a time when he was able

Peter Parks using portable 'snorkel' lens device to film a Portuguese man o' war.

to manoeuvre the camera into a place where hundreds of hammerhead sharks had gathered, only to find them swimming quietly and unhurriedly away into the gloom the moment he pressed the start button. Nevertheless, all who have worked on large-format films agree that the end result is worth the trouble. If you have not watched such a film, imagine a picture the size of the side of an office block, packed with colour and movement. Spectacular ... and it can even be in 3-D.

The film kit for 3-D movie-making is even bulkier. The camera weighs about 600 kg (1300 lb) and all manner of focusing and framing problems are manifest. Put the camera too far from the subject and the audiences have less of a 3-D experience, put it too close and they are overwhelmed by the size of the image. Filmmakers working in 3-D need all the help they can get to put at ease the marine life they are filming. One problem is air bubbles: they frighten everything away.

In order not to disturb animals, underwater camera operators sometimes use what is known as a 're-breather', a modern-day version of the type of breathing apparatus pioneered by Hans Hass all those years ago. It is an almost closed-circuit breathing system that minimizes disturbance, but it does have drawbacks and they can be lethal. Many stories circulate among the diving community of the 'caustic cocktail', but when Howard Hall and Bob Cranston were filming mantis shrimps for a large-format film, *Deep Sea 3-D*, about 20 metres (70 feet) down on the muddy sea floor off Catalina Island, California, the phenomenon became a terrifying reality. With the shot in the can, the equipment was hauled back to the dive boat and

Cameraman Didier Noirot (right) and his re-breather instructor prepare to go under the ice of Lake Baikal in Siberia for Planet Earth.

Howard returned to the surface, making a decompression stop at 4.5 metres (15 feet). Looking above him he saw Bob, who had finished his decompression, bending to put on his flippers. As he straightened up, though, Bob breathed in a highly caustic solution. Earlier in the dive, his full-face mask had leaked and the water had saturated the chemicals in his re-breather, creating a cocktail of salt water and calcium hydroxide that went straight down his throat. In excruciating pain, Bob felt immediately for his emergency buoyancy button and shot to the surface, where he coughed and vomited violently. If he had been in 30 metres (100 feet) of water it could have been fatal. The team had learned a lesson: if water fills the mask when using re-breathers, abort immediately.

Martha and the Helmet of Doom

One piece of kit that magnified all the hazards of working under water was a special helmet developed for the BBC in the 1980s by the French company Laboratoire de Mécanique Appliquée (LAMA) so that presenters could talk to the television audience while under the sea. The thick polycarbonate bubble not only gave the wearer 360-degree visibility looking *out*, but also allowed viewers to look *in*.

The helmet had originally been designed for commercial diving, especially off oil rigs in the North Sea, and had an aural-nasal mask inside the bubble that facilitated breathing. For the television version the mask was removed, so the diver was in a bubble containing not only air to be breathed in but also stale air that had been breathed out. This rendered the diver breathless, making it hard to talk and swim. Too much carbon dioxide also resulted in splitting headaches after dive sessions. Martha Holmes, who first used the device in 1988 in *Reefwatch*, a live outside broadcast from the Red Sea, recalls how sometimes she had a feeling of panic while trying to talk to the camera. She was seen hand-feeding a gigantic Napoleon wrasse with boiled eggs, describing the fish and the experience as it happened, but it is a miracle that she was able to tell us anything at all: she had a serious technical difficulty that was all down to the turn of a screw.

At the back of the helmet is a special screw that controls a valve that fine-tunes the amount of air entering the bubble: too much air and the noise obliterates speech, too little and there is the danger of asphyxiation. *Reefwatch* was co-produced with Israeli television, whose own diver-presenters shared the use of the BBC helmets. Unknown to Martha and her back-up crew, the Israeli hosts had readjusted the screw so that the minimum of air entered the bubble, rather than setting it at the level that the BBC crew had previously found to be comfortable. The consequence

Left: Cameraman Doug Allan films belugas trapped by the ice and attacked by polar bears for Blue Planet.

Right: Presenter Martha Holmes investigates a giant clam while wearing the bubble helmet during the filming of Sea Trek.

was almost fatal. Martha was cued to deliver her first piece to camera live on British television and she took her first deep breath. What flooded the helmet was not air but sea water. The dive was immediately aborted and Martha clambered out and emptied the helmet. Co-host on the dive boat Mike de Gruy had to 'fill' feverishly as Martha dropped back into the water, but the helmet filled with water again. This time Martha flushed the helmet with a forceful jet of air that pushed down the level of the water so that she could speak. She breathed as shallowly as she dared, but as she talked to the TV audience the water level slowly rose again. The dive was aborted a second time. Eventually, soundman Mike Burgess spotted the cause of the problem and the rest of the broadcasts hit the airways without further incidents.

The helmet made another appearance when Martha and Mike de Gruy used it in the award-winning underwater television series *Sea Trek*. They visited such exotic locations as the Great Barrier Reef, the Cayman Islands, California's Channel Islands, the Galapagos and Hawaii and, like *Reefwatch*, the series turned the sea floor into an enormous underwater studio complete with specially designed television cameras, known to the crew as 'aquacams', relaying pictures and sound via fibre-optic video cables directly to a vision-control room on the dive boat. The series saw the intrepid duo hugging stingrays (on their undersides), playing with sea otters, swimming with dolphins and whales, and interacting with inquisitive sharks.

In one sequence, we saw Martha and Mike leaving their protective cage while surrounded by aggressive blue sharks. The sharks circled nervously at first, but gradually gained enough courage to investigate the two 'bubble-headed' sea creatures that had invaded their domain. One shark even 'mouthed' Martha's

polycarbonate sphere – behaviour that under normal circumstances would have resulted in a serious and bloody bite to the head. Protected by the bubble, Martha was able to talk us through what could only be described as a 'nervous moment', although she was more concerned with a gap in the chain-mail suit on her thigh, where the sharks might nibble, than anything that was happening to her helmet.

SEA TREK

One shark even 'mouthed' Martha's polycarbonate sphere – behaviour that under normal circumstances would have resulted in a serious and bloody bite to the head.

For the next life-threatening occurrence, it was Mike de Gruy's turn. He and Martha were under a rock arch, diving to 25 metres (80 feet) – a depth that is comfortable for scuba diving but at the limit for the bubble helmet – when he suddenly ran out of air. His pressure gauge had a screw missing and was spinning freely, so he had no warning. He struck out immediately, finning furiously, but just 2 metres (6 feet) from the surface his progress was halted by the communications cable: it was caught in rocks, preventing him from moving any further. He was in real trouble. It had been nearly a minute since he took his last breath. Then his dive buddy spotted the snagged cable, pulled out the comms plug from his helmet and Mike was able to reach the surface. After that incident a system was devised so that, in an emergency, the bubble-helmet divers could take air from buddies. After *Sea Trek*, though, the helmet was never used again.

HANGING BY A THREAD

During the filming of a sequence for *Abyss–Live*, Mike wore a newer version, the Kirby Morgan 'Movie Helmet', which was linked by an umbilical to the surface ship for air and communications, much as the bubble helmet had been. He was at Cocos Island, off the coast of Costa Rica, swimming with and commentating on a huge school of scalloped hammerhead sharks, when a problem arose. In the strong current, the two boats at the surface broke away from their anchor and Mike drifted off into the Pacific Ocean along with the boat to which he was attached. Eventually, he was hauled to the surface and the boats returned to their original stations.

The *Abyss–Live* programmes also involved diving with deep-sea Russian MIR submersibles. Space was at a premium and director Simon Nash remembers how he, presenter Alastair Fothergill and a Russian pilot had to squeeze into an area no more than 2 metres (6 feet) in diameter. They dived down to 2400 metres (8000 feet) on the Mid-Atlantic Ridge to film 'black smokers' – hot-water vents on the bottom of the deep sea. The dive took 12 hours and the only toilet facility was a plastic bottle. When they returned and were close to the surface, with the expectation of a proper toilet and a cold beer, the submarine started to submerge once more. Simon asked the pilot why they were going back down. 'Small problem,' he replied, breaking a 12-hour silence. The 'small problem' turned out to be a fault in the crane, the only way to haul the 18-tonne sub back on to its mother ship. It was held together by rope. They had to bob around close to the surface until it was fixed.

The Johnson Sealink II submersible used for filming in the deep sea for Blue Planet.

The following year, Simon and Alastair were again in a MIR sub, this time looking for giant tube worms that live next to deep-sea hydrothermal vents. The climax of the sequence was to be a vent packed with life. This time they were deep down in the Pacific and moving into position when they discovered that the vent had stopped gushing. They hastily rewrote the script at 2600 metres (9000 feet), shot the sequence and returned slowly to the surface. This time the rope from the crane kept breaking, leaving them to tumble about inside the sub like 'clothes in a washing machine'.

Staying the right way up was the challenge for cameraman Martin Saunders when filming the underwater sequences in the Arctic for *Kingdom of the Ice Bear*:

'You can't go down under the ice with scuba gear because you blow out bubbles and they wedge under the ice and wipe out whatever you want to film. It looks just like a big mirror. So I had to use surface-breathing apparatus. I was provided with air through a pipe and another pipe took the stale air away. We went out one day for a trial run so I could get used to it. I put on the suit and dropped down through a hole in the ice. One of the main things you have to do with these suits is to control the buoyancy, so I'd let the air out and I'd sink down. Then I'd fill up the suit with air and I'd rise and crash into the underside of the ice. One time I was wedged under the ice because I'd let too much air into the suit and my legs started to float up, so I was pinned horizontally underneath the ice, not able to move this way or that. I shut all the valves, took stock of the situation and decided to let the air out. But the air goes out from the head end of the suit first, so my head became less buoyant and sank. This meant that I was standing upside down under the ice!'

Martin eventually managed to work his way round so he was the right way up and he went on to get amazing pictures of seals and walruses under water.

It is an adventure that never stops. At the time of writing, Charles Maxwell tells of his most recent experiences at Dyer Island, free-diving and filming with great white sharks for French television. He was in the water with presenter Nicolas Hulot and marine biologist Laurent Ballesta, waiting desperately for the critical shot, but the sharks kept their distance. Just as the team were making for the dive boat, however, a large great white suddenly turned sharply and sped towards them. Charles swung the camera to frame the shot, but realized his two companions had not seen the shark approaching. In that split second, which seemed like minutes, he had to decide whether to film them or warn them. Fortunately, Laurent spotted the shark and grabbed Nicolas' arm. With less than 1 metre (3 feet) to spare, the shark veered away and swam, quite literally, into the setting sun. Charles got his shot.

Camerman Doug Allan films under the sea ice in Lancaster Sound, Canadian Arctic.

BLUE PLANET

DESCRIBED AS 'the definitive exploration of the Earth's final frontier', *Blue Planet* lived up to expectations. Led by one-time head of the NHU Alastair Fothergill, the production team scoured the world's oceans for stories and pictures that would reveal the underwater realm as it had never been seen before. They used satellite tracking to find and film the largest animal that has ever lived – the blue whale – in the Pacific Ocean; followed the extraordinary sardine run and its procession of sharks, dolphins and seabirds off the South African coast; witnessed the heart-rending death of a baby grey whale pursued by orcas off California; and watched as 5000 sea turtles hauled their bulk up beaches in Costa Rica during the *arribada* or mass nesting.

Patience had to be a watchword on this series, and producer Andy Byatt knows more than most what waiting can mean. On and off, it took four years of scanning an empty ocean before he nailed the sequence he needed, on the very last day of filming. He was rewarded with a writhing bait ball being herded by blue marlin. Then yellowfin tuna slammed into the fish, picking them off one by one, and finally a Brydes whale took the remaining shoal in one enormous gulp, the first time that such an event had been filmed under water. Underwater cameraman Doug Anderson, snorkelling at the time, had to hold his breath for over a minute while the enormous whale passed within only a few metres of him.

Cameraman Simon King films a flatback turtle on Crab Island, Queensland, Australia.

Diving on reefs at night revealed how whitetip reef sharks hunt in complete darkness; polecams were used to show Pacific porbeagle sharks chasing salmon, and re-breathers enabled cameramen to get close to thousands of schooling hammerhead and silky sharks without scaring them away. Diving research vehicles, such as the Johnson Sealink minisub, took cameraman Mike de Gruy to film a bizarre 'lake' 1500 metres (1 mile) down at the bottom of the Gulf of Mexico; and high-definition pictures from the twilight zone 4500 metres (nearly 15,000 feet) down in the deep sea not only delighted television audiences worldwide but also formed a valuable resource to be brooded over by oceanographers from the world's major marine laboratories.

[CHAPTER NINE]

New Science

Wildlife filmmakers travel to the world's most inaccessible places and use such sophisticated lenses and cameras that they chance upon things that might otherwise be overlooked. They encounter new species yet to be described for science, observe behaviour that has never been seen before and create a permanent record. In this way, they can give something back to the scientific community – and they have been doing so since the earliest days of wildlife filmmaking. ☞

Above: The Costa Rican tiny golden toad, extinct since 1989.

New Species and New Discoveries

Lemurs such as the indris and sifaka were filmed for the first time for David Attenborough's *Zoo Quest to Madagascar,* the footage adding greatly to the little that was known at the time about these rare creatures. The same has been true of many films from that day to this. *Trials of Life* executive producer Peter Jones, in East Africa with the distinguished big cat researcher Craig Packer, had first-hand experience of how filmmakers can help the academics. On their return to base each evening the film crew would tell the scientists about what they had seen during the day.

'On one occasion,' Peter recalled, 'we were filming amongst the great zebra herds on the Serengeti when we saw an unusual example of infanticide. A stallion, which had just taken over a group of females, was worrying a pregnant female. He was jostling and mounting her and generally making life difficult for her, and eventually brought on the premature birth of her calf, which died. All the evidence indicated that this was a deliberate form of infanticide practised by the stallion. When we returned to camp and told Packer about the day's events, he declared, "I'm going to give up doing my research here and just go out with a BBC film crew, because it seems every time you go out you stumble into something quite fascinating."'

Above: Effect of supernormal stimulus – the gull chick prefers the pencil with many dots to the model gull with only one spot.

Opposite: David Attenborough with a titan arum in Sumatra for Private Life of Plants.

Roger Jackman, one of the cameramen on *The Living Planet,* stumbled across a frog in Brunei that lived beside a waterfall. Most male frogs croak to attract a mate, but here the crashing water would have drowned any sounds this little character made. Instead, it flashed a blue foot, behaviour that was quite new to science.

Roger did it again when working with Professor Tom Eisner of Cornell University on the award-winning *Secret Weapons* for *Natural World*. Their team was looking for bombardier beetles at night when Roger heard a faint scream.

'I couldn't work out what it was. I couldn't see anything in the dark, but used my torch to look around a pond and could see a number of toadlets. They were young spadefoot toads beginning to emerge from the water. I thought the noise must have been something to do with them, but what? I searched around the pool and then spotted one as its head disappeared under the mud. I immediately dug my hand into the mud and discovered a huge fly larva that had caught the toadlet and was dragging it down to feed on it. What we discovered later is that the larvae harpoon passing toads, drag them under the mud and suck them dry. There was a whole layer under the surface containing the carcasses of toadlets.'

Tom Eisner, who had initially been rather annoyed that Roger was more interested in the pond than in searching for bombardier beetles, was intrigued enough to pursue the new discovery. The result was a scientific paper in which Roger was cited as a co-author.

More than a decade later, *The Private Life of Plants* continued this tradition when the film crew covering the Borneo rainforest noticed semicircular pieces missing from the leaves of ginger plants, similar to the damage made by leaf-cutter bees. Closer inspection revealed that the fragments were not severed completely, but had been fashioned into miniature domes on the underside of the leaves. The crew gently peeled back a tiny flap and discovered a minuscule caterpillar hiding there, so they took a bunch of leaves and caterpillars back to their hotel in order to obtain a time-lapse sequence of them constructing their domes. It was not until they returned to Bristol and the film had been processed, however, that the detail could be seen. Each caterpillar made two circular cuts in the edge of the leaf and then spun a hinge of silk. As the silk dried, the flap of leaf was pulled around it and the tiny

David Attenborough filming for Living Planet *on the beach.*

house completed, with the little caterpillar tucked safely inside. It was behaviour that had never been seen before.

Another sequence in *The Private Life of Plants* explained how a pitcher plant's pitcher developed, something that had not previously been seen in such detail. And in the same series, David Attenborough was taken to the rainforest of Sumatra to find the world's biggest flower with an unbranched inflorescence, the titan arum. As its scientific name, *Amorphophallus titanium*, suggests, it is a huge phallus-shaped structure about 3 metres (10 feet) tall. You might think that such a large flower would be easy to find, but the titan arum flower lasts for only three or four days, so experts from the Netherlands and USA were asked to help find one. After much searching, they succeeded. The air reeked of decaying flesh, the means by which the plant attracts the insects that help its pollination. It was the first time anybody had filmed the flowers and their pollinators at work, and it gave rise to another revelation. The textbooks of the time referred to beetles attending the giant flowers, but while the crew was filming on the second day they noticed that the main visitors were sweat bees ... and a new species to boot.

LIFE OF BIRDS

When food is in short supply, coot chicks begging for food are pecked on the head by their parents. After a sustained battering, the chicks stop begging and starve to death.

CRIMINAL COOTS AND CLEVER CROWS

The Life of Birds made new discoveries, too. The team was able to confirm that on town and country ponds throughout the United Kingdom child abuse and even infanticide are being committed. When food is in short supply, coot chicks begging for food are pecked on the head by their parents. After a sustained battering, the chicks stop begging and starve to death. Cameraman Barrie Britton caught the behaviour on film on an Oxfordshire pond. Nobody had believed it happened until he came back with the pictures.

Another first for *The Life of Birds* was the courtship dance of Alaska's buff-breasted sandpiper, an event that takes place on just four days in the year, immediately after the birds arrive from their migration north. It had never been filmed before and had been seen for the first time by ornithologist Rick Lanctot, who was studying the birds, only a short while before Barrie Britton and Miles Barton arrived to film another species not far away. Rick alerted the production team to the birds' arrival and they debated whether to finish what they were filming or to drop everything and go. They chose the latter and headed out to the sandpipers. What they saw at first was a rather dull-looking bird, but then it started its display.

'A male raised one wing in salute, the displaying began and Barrie started filming,' recalled Miles. 'The male waves at the females and, once he has an audience, he extends both wings wide and points his beak skywards. He reveals white wing flashes rather in the manner of a streetseller opening his raincoat to reveal dodgy watches. The females lunge forwards and eventually in the mêlée he gets to mate with one.

'Everything went right. We were able to approach close to the birds, so busy were they with their displaying. We filmed from about two in the afternoon until eleven at night, taking full advantage of the long Arctic summer daylight. We noticed a bank of cloud on the horizon; half an hour later it was overhead and we began to pack up. As we walked back, it closed in completely and became so thick we could barely find the truck. We were fogged in for a week and by the time it had cleared the display was over for another year.'

A colleague in Japanese television relayed another curious piece of behaviour to Miles and his team. There were reports that carrion crows had learned to use cars as nutcrackers, so Miles and Barrie arrived in Japan full of anticipation. However, their hosts admitted they had not seen the behaviour recently, so what were they to do? Well, they went and sat beside the road in the most likely places. Students also stationed themselves around the city, but after a couple of days of being asphyxiated by carbon monoxide fumes at busy crossings, they still had not seen anything remotely significant. Then they had a report from a local driving school and went along to have a look. They found an enclosed area of tarmac laid out with crossings, lights and other street features.

'There I saw crows flying up into the air and not only dropping nuts, but also following them down on to the tarmac,' said Miles. 'I had to buy the driving-school manager a large, well-decorated cake – the correct protocol – and we were allowed to film for a few days, but it was all to no avail; they stopped doing it. Then, two days before we were to return home, we heard from a student who had witnessed the elusive behaviour at a pedestrian crossing.

'We immediately went down there and, as it was raining off and on, Barrie put up his hide to protect his camera equipment. It was rather ridiculous considering the tameness of the birds and the setting, and a policeman arrived to complain about the obstruction. We had to buy red triangle signs to place in front and behind, but finally we were allowed to film the crows. They flew up on to the traffic lights with a nut in their beaks and then dropped the nut into the oncoming traffic.

Once the nut was crushed under a wheel, the crow waited for the traffic lights to go red and the traffic to stop, and then it would fly down to pick up the pieces amongst the pedestrians on the crossing.'

In the same series, another member of the crow family, the Caledonian crow, was seen using tools to extract grubs from trees, something that was relatively new to science and thought to be impossible to film. The team not only recorded the behaviour, but also included a view from inside the tree, which showed the precise way in which the crow used its tool – a revelation even to the scientists who had been studying it.

Waiting for Proof

David Attenborough's invertebrate series *Life in the Undergrowth* was able to confirm another scientist's observations. Her subjects were ants, and they were fastidious in the way they cleared part of the forest by poisoning plants that were not useful to them. Still frames from the film supported the researcher's paper when it was published in the learned scientific journal *Nature*. It was the first time the detail of the behaviour had been caught on camera.

And, bringing the custom right up to date, Sir David's new series *Life in Cold Blood* has uncovered previously unknown behaviour exhibited by caecilians. These are legless amphibians resembling worms that spend most of their time underground, and the young of some species feed on the skin of their mother. Series producer Hilary Jeffkins and cameraman Alastair McEwan travelled to Brazil, hoping to film this behaviour, but when they arrived the scientist they were visiting announced that he had never seen this in the species he was studying. Undeterred, Hilary and Alastair camped out in the laboratory, literally, and waited ... and waited. Eventually their patience paid off. They not only filmed the tiny caecilians stripping the special layer of skin from their mother's body, but also discovered that she produces a secretion that appears to attract them to her ... all in a species thought not to exhibit the behaviour. The babies performed for only a few hours, so if Hilary and Alastair had not kept vigil all night they would have missed them altogether and science would have been the poorer for it.

This is a pattern that repeats itself time and time again. An episode of *Alien Empire* followed up an observation by a researcher in Costa Rica that few of her peers had believed at first. She saw a species of assassin bug actually using a 'tool'. The bug caught a termite, sucked it dry and then, like a human angler dangling a bait, used the dried skin to 'fish' for more termites. The NHU crew filmed the entire event, proving that the entomologist had been right all along.

Cameraman Mike Richards is watched by elephant seals while he films king penguins for Life in the Freezer, *on South Georgia.*

Another cameraman, working in the Amazon, spotted a leaf that was floating upstream. He jumped into the water, caught the leaf and discovered that underneath was a fish. It was using the leaf as a parasol, not only to hide from fish-eating birds but also to help it to sneak up on its own prey. When a scientist at the Natural History Museum in London saw the footage he realized that the fish was totally new to science, too.

The way that Antarctic fur seals feed on krill had always puzzled scientists and, when an underwater film cameraman was sent to South Georgia for *Life in the Freezer*, the filmmakers were able to show what really went on. Krill, it seems, form great shoals at depth in the Southern Ocean, but the seals round them up and force them towards the surface. The seals could be seen manoeuvring around the edges of the krill balls and then swimming upwards, following a spiralling path and feeding as they went. By trapping the krill against the surface, they provide easy prey not only for themselves, but also for the many surface-feeding birds, such as albatrosses, that feed on krill too.

Rarely Seen

Wildlife on One was responsible for many revelations. While filming *Bodysnatchers* for the series, producer Keenan Smart and army-ant expert Nigel Franks went in search of ant-cleaning stations. They had read about them in Victorian accounts, but Nigel had not witnessed them himself. Army-ant soldiers have such large and powerful jaws that they cannot clean themselves, and Victorian naturalists had noted that smaller workers cleaned their pincers for them. Keenan searched and searched, and finally succeeded in proving that the Victorian observers had been right all along. *Reef Encounter* revealed that sea turtles – like sharks, rays and groupers – also visit 'cleaning stations' where they are attended by cleaner fish and shrimps.

Earwig showed earwigs flying, a phenomenon that is mentioned in the textbooks but is rarely seen, the last record having been 50 years previously; and *Possums: Tale of the Unexpected* focused on the feeding behaviour of Australia's striped possum. It extracts grubs from rotting wood, but until producer Karen Bass and her film crew came along nobody had seen how it winkled them out. They discovered that the possum first taps its finger along the branch, testing for hollow places, and, having found a likely spot, chisels away at the bark with its front teeth to make an entry hole. It then pushes in its slender tongue to taste for grubs, but not to extract them. The extraction is achieved by an especially elongated index finger. When the film was viewed some time later, the team also noticed that the finger must be 'double-jointed', for it could move in almost any direction in order to extract the grub. It was another first, and it prompted another scientific paper.

The film crew in Gabon for Bernard Walton's *Mandrills: Painted Faces of the Forest* came across the unexpected sight of thousands of river martins swirling in a great black cloud, before they settled down to roost close to the river. Although it wasn't on the schedule, Bernard decided to film the flock; when he returned to Bristol he discovered that this was the largest concentration of river martins in the world. Swallows and martins expert Angela Turner saw the sequence:

'It was known that martins breed and migrate in large groups, but roosting behaviour has not been described or at least not in much detail. So I was not expecting to see such a large flock or to see it flying in formation like that. Many species of swallows do typically form large flocks and wheel about in the sky before entering a roost, but river martins are in a separate subfamily of the swallow and martin family, so I didn't necessarily expect them to behave in a similar way. The martins are interesting because, although well known to local people, they aren't well known to Western scientists. There are odd bits of information about them, but no good study.'

WILDLIFE ON ONE

Reef Encounter *revealed that sea turtles – like sharks, rays and groupers – also visit 'cleaning stations' where they are attended by cleaner fish and shrimps.*

In *Malice in Wonderland*, a flock of a different kind caught the attention of watching scientists. It had long been known that small birds will gang up and mob a larger intruder, but not that fish do the same thing. The programme showed how a species of reef fish – *Anthias* spp. – mobs larger predatory fish. Similarly, *Wildlife Special: Great White Shark* featured seals at Dyer Island, South Africa, actually mobbing the largest and most powerful shark in the sea. The film also showed how great whites display to each other and revealed their tactic for sneaking up on unwary prey. Several of the film crew and the film's scientific adviser are to be credited in scientific papers arising directly from behaviour they captured on film.

Shooting with specialist cameras at night has been especially fruitful. In *Wildlife Special: Crocodile*, a sequence with Nile crocodiles in East Africa showed that, contrary to popular belief, they hunt at night and mainly chase fish rather than larger, warm-blooded prey. A night shoot in *Wildlife Special: Leopard* revealed how the animal reduces the sound it makes by putting its rear paw in exactly the same place that the front paw has gone before, while keeping its eyes fixed firmly on the prey it is stalk-

Richard Kirby trying to capture the hatching of baby Nile crocodiles in Natal, South Africa. The mother is close, and at this time is most protective and potentially aggressive.

ing. Scientists wondered whether it looked down to check the position of its feet, but the night-vision camera showed otherwise. In the film the leopard never takes its eyes away from its target. It gently slides its rear foot forward, feels for the imprint made by its front paw and, with remarkable precision, places it on the exact same spot.

A word of warning, however. Do not believe *everything* you see on the screen. There is the classic tale of an ornithologist who wanted to calculate the speed at which a peregrine stooped and, having seen on television a film showing a peregrine doing just that, he wrote to the BBC requesting a copy. One was duly dispatched and the scientist set about his calculations. He came up with a speed that beggared belief, much faster than anybody had ever dreamed possible. There was, however, a fundamental flaw. The film was so well crafted that the scientist had failed to notice the stooping flight had been edited!

TRIALS OF LIFE

THE THIRD PART of David Attenborough's 'Life Trilogy' was the acclaimed 12-part series *Trials of Life* (1990). While *Life on Earth* had given an evolutionary view of animals and *Living Planet* had considered habitats, *Trials of Life* focused on animal behaviour. It was the first major NHU series to work closely with ethologists – researchers engaged in the scientific study of animal behaviour – and indeed, research for the programmes was so extensive, including blanket coverage of international animal research conferences for news of all the latest developments, that it was over 18 months before any film went through the camera. The entire production period was three and a half years.

David Attenborough with red crabs on Christmas Island.

Each programme featured a different aspect of the journey animals make through life – from birth to adulthood and the continuation of species. What the programmes were able to reveal astounded television audiences everywhere. Thanks to the research of Christophe Boesch and Hedwige Boesch-Acherman in the Tai Forest of the Cote d'Ivoire, the general public saw for the first time that chimpanzees were fierce hunters and meat-eaters. Cynthia Moss, who had worked with elephants in East Africa for over a quarter of a century, advised on how the crew could be in the right place at the right time to film the more intimate moments of elephant behaviour. A special probe lens or endoscope was used to take the viewer inside the bivouac of army ants in Panama with the help of Professor Nigel Franks, now at the University of Bristol, and thanks to a closely studied group of Florida scrub jays in the USA, a bird was able to land right on cue on Sir David Attenborough's hand. And who could forget the killer whales surfing right up on to beaches in Patagonia to pluck fur seals from the shoreline or the tiger sharks ambushing albatross chicks on one of the Hawaiian islands?

[CHAPTER TEN]

Making a Difference

In the early days of wildlife filmmaking, attitudes to wild animals and wild places were quite different from what they are today. Filmmakers paid little heed to the welfare of the beasts they were filming; rather, they seemed to take particular delight in killing them. In 1884, for example, Eadweard Muybridge had a tiger attack an old buffalo at Philadelphia Zoo; and in 1903 the inventor Thomas Edison's bizarrely titled *Electrocuting an Elephant* showed Topsy, an elephant who had killed one of her keepers, being executed at Luna Park on Coney Island, New York, in front of a paying audience. ☞

Above: Elephants travel in the remote Namib desert.

Changing Attitudes

The things people did for the sake of the camera were astounding. In 1910, Carl Akeley hired a tribe of local hunters to kill a lion in the traditional way with spears. The good people obliged, but it took him three weeks and 14 lions before he felt he had what he wanted. When the film was processed, however, none of the shots were any good. Fourteen lions had died for nothing. Akeley tried again in 1926, on a filming expedition in Africa with Martin and Osa Johnson. On this occasion, the lion was clearly tethered. In the Johnsons' *Congrilla* (1932), publicized as the 'first sound from darkest Africa', the couple were seen capturing and hog-tying a pair of terrified baby gorillas. Many other films showed the hunting and killing of animals.

Films were also loose with the truth. In 1930, *Africa Speaks* had African-American 'hunters' walking in front of back-projected pictures of savannah or jungle in a Hollywood studio, but the publicity claimed they had been filmed in Africa. In view of this fraud, Theodore Roosevelt, introducing Cherry Kearton's films in New York in 1913, had to make a point of telling the audience that they were not faked.

Looking back at the history of wildlife filming shows how attitudes have changed, not only in filmmaking but also in the general community. Hunting animals with guns gradually gave way to hunting them with cameras. The early films of David Attenborough and Gerald Durrell, among others, followed zoo-collecting

Gerald Durrell's early films followed his animal-collecting expeditions, a type of wildlife film that would unlikely be made today.

expeditions, something that zoos do not do any more. Even if they did, today's wildlife filmmakers would probably not film them, although the 'round-em-up-and-ship-em-out' films showing the translocation of animals from one park to another seem to have taken their place.

Sense and Sensationalism

Other things have changed, too. For fear of offending their audiences, the earliest films were very cautious about showing mating activity; today people recognize it as an essential part of animal life. Nevertheless, it was not until 1983 that television in the USA first showed mating animals, when Marty Stoufer included a scene of pigs copulating in an episode of *Wild America*. The sequence was in the master tapes and aired on most stations ... but some local affiliates still removed it.

Filmmakers are also more cautious about the way animals are handled. As late as the 1950s they continued to take enormous liberties in order to make animals behave in the way they thought was suitable for their films. Today, the audience is much more sophisticated and does not accept that kind of manipulation. By and large, wildlife filmmakers are also now very honest. If they use techniques that are not purely observational, an accompanying 'making of' type of programme comes clean about how some sequences were achieved.

Nevertheless, unscrupulous filmmakers will go to great lengths to sensationalize events and not reveal how it was done – and this charge is not confined to the early pioneers. In a polar bear film produced in the 1980s, for example, the filmmakers placed themselves inside a cage to film the bears around them. The bears are seen trying to get at the person inside ... or at least that is what they look as if they are doing. In reality, the filmmakers had spread fish oil on the bars of the cage and the bears were simply licking it off. The truth had been bent for effect, and the consequence could well have been that bears were considered a greater menace than they really were and shot unnecessarily.

> *As late as the 1950s filmmakers continued to take enormous liberties in order to make animals behave in the way they thought was suitable for their films.*

In 1986, in a film by George James and Brian Vallee called *Cruel Camera*, the Canadian Broadcasting Corporation gathered together some of the questionable sequences involving animals. It shows cruelty – how in some early westerns, for example, horses died or were brought down by tripwires – but it also shows outright fraud. A popular American wildlife series is castigated for faking scenes, such as pitting an alligator against a water moccasin tethered by its tail and thrown repeatedly into the set, or 'rescuing' a bear from a swamp after it had been pushed in and was frightened half to death. And the lemming suicide scene in Walt Disney's *White Wilderness* (see Chapter One) is now legendary.

In both the USA and the UK, legislation to protect animals was brought in at an early stage. In the UK, the Cinematography Film (Animals) Act became law in 1937; thanks to the US Animal Humane Society similar laws were already in place when the early westerns were made, but producers circumvented them by filming in countries such as Spain, which had yet to make their activities illegal. Today, the industry has a voluntary code of conduct and is keen to ensure that animals are not harmed in any way or disturbed unnecessarily, so the ethics of wildlife filmmaking are frequently debated at international gatherings. Early in the industry's history, the use of tethered animals as stool pigeons to attract predators was condemned outright, and today the unofficial watchdogs are quick to call foul at the slightest hint of prey being fed to predators or animals being tethered or restrained. The ethical debate is ongoing. Currently, the way in which some presenters interact with animals, such as jumping on crocodiles or wrestling with snakes, is being questioned – just how far can programme-makers go in the name of 'edu-tainment'? Some argue that animal wrangling is one way to attract attention and get youngsters switched on to wildlife, while others see it as an unacceptable face of filmmaking. Individual filmmakers can, of course, follow what they feel is right or wrong, what is legal or illegal, but in the end the viewer decides by changing channels or reaching for the 'off' button.

Currently, the way in which some presenters interact with animals, such as jumping on crocodiles or wrestling with snakes, is being questioned – just how far can programme-makers go in the name of 'edu-tainment'?

Report or Crusade

Marketing, though, can taint viewer response, with unexpected results. The most extraordinary campaign ever must be Time-Life's promotion of the *Trials of Life* videos in the USA. The series was a serious look at animal behaviour, presented by David Attenborough, but it was marketed as sex, violence, blood and gore in a commercial that ended with the immortal words 'Find out why we call them animals!' It became a bestseller.

More usually, wildlife films are less in your face and audiences seem to prefer it that way. Audience research directed at BBC wildlife films broadcast in the UK consistently returns an 'appreciation score' (how viewers rate a programme shown as a percentage) way above those of other genres. Taking an arbitrary day in May 2007, the average score for non-wildlife shows was 74, whereas nature programmes averaged 86. Audience figures are high, too. A recorded 9.4 million people in Britain watched the first episode of *Planet Earth* in 2006, and most of them stayed with it until the end of the series. *Springwatch* wiped light entertainment competition off the board. Even with a plethora of alternative channels, people turned on to watch wildlife.

With audiences like that, not only in the UK but all over the world, the potential for putting over a conservation message is enormous. The dilemma, though, has been whether television should report or crusade.

One of the first big conservation statements was made in the late 1950s. Alan Root was working with Armand and Michaela Denis when a zebra-striped Dornier aircraft flew in and landed close to the Serengeti park headquarters. Out stepped Bernard and Michael Grzimek, father and son, the father already a distinguished zoologist in his native Germany. They wanted to make a film about the great herds of wildebeest and zebra that cross the Serengeti Plains, one stage in the fight to ensure that the boundaries of the national park encompassed the animals' great migration. Alan and Michael hit it off. They had the same sense of dedication and of fun. But tragedy struck when Michael's plane hit a flying vulture and plunged to the ground, killing him instantly. His grave is on the rim of the Ngorongoro Crater in Tanzania; his headstone carries the epitaph, 'He gave all he possessed for the wild animals of Africa, including his life.'

Alan Root and Bernhard Grzimek completed the film, shooting in colour on 35mm. Released in 1959 under the title *Serengeti Shall Not Die*, it was awarded an Oscar® for best documentary (feature) and became one of the first films to raise world awareness of the need for wildlife conservation.

That same year, the BBC aired its own first conservation film, *The Return of the Osprey*, recounting the success the RSPB was having in protecting the nest of a pair of ospreys at Loch Garton. The conservation message was frequently put over in Peter Scott's *Look;* and in the autumn of 1961 an international conference in Arusha, Tanzania, saw Scott at centre stage in the setting up of the World Wildlife Fund. The conference also prompted a special season of conservation films, including Bernard

Grzimek's *No Room for Wild Animals*. In 1966, *Look* gave viewers a hint of more things to come with an extended edition simply called *Living with Nature*. The distinguished guest was HRH The Duke of Edinburgh and the theme was nature in cities. The NHU was already in the vanguard of the conservation movement.

The tradition carried into the 1980s with a *Look* look-alike, the natural history magazine *Nature*, presented live on BBC2 by Tony Soper. From its outset it introduced conservation issues. Admittedly they were snuck in with a sugar-coating of pure natural history, but the early programmes laid the foundations for the fully fledged conservation series that *Nature* became. Acid rain, air quality, fisheries, rabies and the trade in bush meat all became prime-time topics on BBC2, with a special series on *The State of Europe* in 1989.

An Extraordinary Privilege

A single film showing the fragility of living systems was, and still is, a rarity in the television schedules. One of the exceptions came in 1981 with Phil Agland's *Korup*. It explored one of the last swathes of African rainforest – in southwestern Cameroon – and showed it as a single living organism: take any one thing away and the whole ecosystem collapses. Every plant and animal in the forest is as important as its neighbour, no matter how big or small. *Korup* was one of a series of stunningly beautiful conservation films under the umbrella title *Fragile Earth*, produced by Mike Rosenberg's Partridge Films in the early 1980s and including Alan MacGregor's *Pantanal*, John Waters' *Alyeska*, Richard Foster's *Selva Verde Central American Rainforest* and Phil Agland's *Siarau: The Tidal Forest* and *Kalahari: Wilderness Without Water*.

Phil Aglund leaving the African rainforest.

There was, however, a trend in the 1970s and 1980s for almost every blue-chip wildlife film to show a particular species or habitat and then, at the very end, introduce the conservation coda, 'Sorry, folks, but it's all going to disappear!' Viewers and channel controllers alike soon found this drip-feed approach tiresome and there was a period when conservation films were firmly labelled 'doom and gloom' and began to vanish from the schedules.

David Attenborough did not subscribe to this school of thought. His philosophy has always been simple: show people the beauty and awesomeness of nature and it should go some way to helping them care about it. In the radio programme *You Should Have Been Here Yesterday*, David Attenborough outlined his guiding principle.

'I have always thought that we are extraordinarily privileged to make films for television, in that we have this stage, which is watched by 10 million people, and we are allowed to occupy it for maybe an hour a week. We have to be very careful that we do not abuse that privilege by turning it always into propaganda. It doesn't mean that you don't sometimes grind your axe, because you sometimes do, but not continuously. Secondly, if people think conservation is important and that plants and animals should survive, they have to be convinced that those species are worth preserving. You mustn't go on all the time and say, "This is endangered, therefore conserve", before you actually reveal or display what this is. So seeing the natural world and becoming aware of the complexities, beauty and importance of the natural world is one of the major things that television should do. I'm encouraged in this belief because the change in people's attitude towards the natural world over the past 50 years has been fantastic. The policy to that degree has worked.'

David Attenborough is dwarfed by a saguaro cactus while filming The Private Life of Plants.

The response worldwide to David Attenborough's many landmark series certainly bears this out. Everywhere they have been shown, they have had a demonstrable impact. In Italy, for example, where there was a tradition of shooting just about anything that moved, especially birds, these films are credited with a significant shift in public attitude that began to nurture a conservation ethos.

At the start of the new millennium, however, David Attenborough came out of the conservation closet and made the three-part series *State of the Planet*. It showed the world as it really is, warts and all. In an interview included in the BBC website accompanying the series, David Attenborough posed an important question:

Opposite: David Attenborough and king penguins during the filming of Life in the Freezer.

Left: David Attenborough rides an Asian elephant in Thailand during the filming of The Life of Mammals.

'The question is, are we happy to suppose that our grandchildren may never be able to see an elephant except in a picture book? And if the answer is no, then people worldwide have got to say: "Yes, elephants are a glory and a splendour and a wonder and we should not be responsible for their disappearance; and we are prepared to do something about it."'

'It seems to me that the natural world is the greatest source of excitement; the greatest source of visual beauty; the greatest source of intellectual interest. It is the greatest source of so much in life that makes life worth living.'

Local, National, Global

Are We Changing Planet Earth? and *Can We Save Planet Earth?*, a two-part collaboration between the BBC's science and natural history departments in 2006, marked the first time that David Attenborough had publicly voiced his concerns about the impact of global warming. In them he declared that climate change was 'the biggest challenge facing the world' and that 'scientific data clearly showed that climate change was beyond doubt'. The programmes were followed a year later by *Climate Change – Britain Under Threat*, a co-production between the BBC and the Open University that looked at the way things might change in the UK.

Elsewhere in the world, wildlife films are also having an impact. Indian filmmaker Mike Pandey's powerful, Wildscreen Panda-winning film *Shores of Silence* (2000), for example, has resulted in a change in his country's law. The first film to highlight the massacre of whale sharks along Indian coasts, it took three years to make and showed whale sharks being hauled from the water and butchered on the beach, their fins sold for shark-fin soup and their liver oil used to waterproof boats. But Mike did not release his film immediately after gathering the images of the carnage. He wanted to show a balanced picture, weighing the benefits to the fishermen against the damage to whale shark populations. In the process, he discovered a new aspect to the dilemma and introduced the notion that the tourist potential of whale sharks greatly outweighed their value as shark-fin soup. He showed the film first to local fishing communities, who had not realized they were destroying such an impressive animal – they immediately wanted to help change things. Mike then showed the film to the state government, which responded by giving the whale shark legal protection.

Mike followed this with a film about those unlovable beasts, the vultures. At one time, India had the highest density of vultures in the world – an estimated 85 million of them – but in recent years a staggering 99 per cent have disappeared, mostly due to a veterinary drug picked up when scavenging from cow carcasses. Publicity for the film has highlighted the problem and has helped to speed up the drug's withdrawal.

'We can make a difference, locally, nationally and globally,' says Mike. 'Sometimes it takes nations and decades to bring about change and sometimes – as we have shown – changes take place when we touch the hearts and minds of people.'

On a smaller scale, this sentiment has been evident in the UK. After BBC2's *Britain Goes Wild* in 2004, the RSPB sold out of nest boxes and the demand for bee boxes was so high that the manufacturers had to work through the night for several weeks to meet it. The day after the first series of *Elephant Diaries* was transmitted in 2005, a UK-based elephant charity was richer to the tune of £10,000 and gained over a thousand new members. And during the fortnight after the first showing of BBC1's early evening prime-time *Orang-utan Diaries* in 2007, the charity involved received more than £100,000 in online donations.

Television *has* been making a difference.

SAVING PLANET EARTH

IN AN UNPRECEDENTED season of programmes on BBC1 and BBC2, and associated events such as vodcasts, demonstrating how conservation can make a difference, the BBC has established the BBC Wildlife Fund, a registered charity which is to distribute money raised by donations from members of the public to help support projects protecting the world's endangered wildlife. Television programmes in which celebrities met endangered 'stars' from the natural world culminated in a televised fund-raising event at the Royal Botanic Gardens, Kew, hosted by popular television presenters Alan Titchmarsh and Graham Norton. The films featured nine endangered animals and related conservation projects – wandering albatross, Siamese crocodile, desert elephant, lowland gorilla, orangutan, Indian rhino, Bengal tiger, Sri Lankan sea turtle and the Ethiopian wolf – with a further 14 selected for future attention. Regional television and local radio joined forces with the NHU to highlight UK-based projects, while children's television took young viewers to the ends of the Earth to see for themselves the dangers facing animals and the projects designed to conserve them.

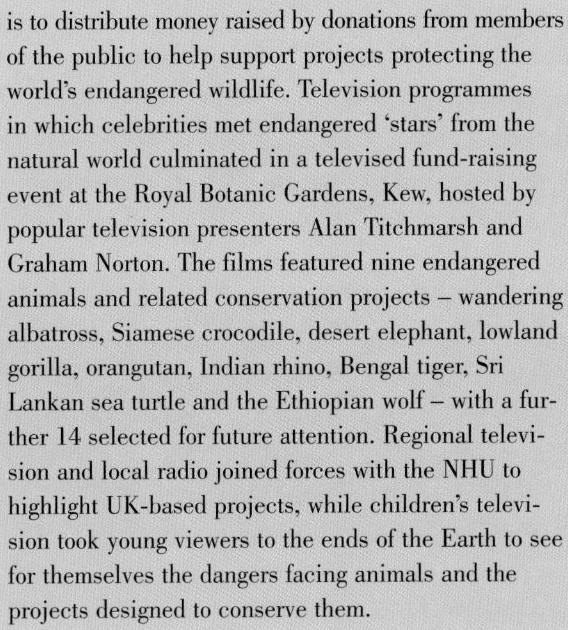

It was the first time that the BBC had used a series of this kind to raise funds for conservation, using the precedent set by its Children in Need and Comic Relief appeals.

Donations can be made to:
BBC Wildlife Fund
PO Box 60905
London W12 7UU

Or call the donation phone line 08705-100-700. Or visit the web page http://www.bbc.co.uk/savingplanetearth/

Will Young and Carol Thatcher participate in Saving Planet Earth.

Acknowledgements

I WOULD LIKE TO THANK all the dedicated filmmakers who helped me to compile this brief account of wildlife filmmaking's first hundred years. Their anecdotes bring to life what could otherwise have been a dry history. So, in alphabetical order, a big 'thank you' to: Pelham Aldrich-Blake, Doug Allan, Paul Appleby, Sir David Attenborough, Melinda Barker, Miles Barton, Jen and Des Bartlett, Karen Bass, Peter Bassett, Stephen Bolwell, James Brickell, Clare Brook, Andrew Buchanan, Martyn Colbeck, Huw Cordey, Peter Crawford, Jean Paul Davidson, Sue Flood, Richard Ganniclift, Mike de Gruy, Howard Hall, Martyn Harries, Jean Hartley, Martha Holmes, Roger Jackman, Hilary Jeffkins, Peter Jones, Amanda Kear, Lionel Kelloway, Neil Lucas, Tim Martin, Charles Maxwell, Hugh Miles, Simon Nash, Steve Nichols, Barry Paine, Nigel Pope, Robin Prytherch, Alan Root, Mike Rosenberg, Mike Salisbury OBE, Martin Saunders, Tim Scoones, Martin Shann, Keenan Smart, Tony Soper and John Sparks. I would also like to acknowledge the help of those who are sadly no longer with us but who had earlier recounted their stories and experiences, including Desmond Hawkins, Hugo van Lawick, and Christopher Parsons OBE. Thank you also to Alison Tunnicliffe, Lucie Muir, Derek Kilkenny-Blake, Richard Edwards and Harriet Nimmo at Wildscreen in Bristol for help with sourcing photographs, and to Caroline Taggart, Eleanor Maxfield, Lisa Pettibone and Shirley Patton at BBC Books for turning my humble meanderings into an attractive and readable book.

Further Reading

Attenborough, David (2002) *Life on Air*, BBC Books, London.
Bousé, Derek (2000)*Wildlife Films*, University of Pennsylvania Press; Philadelphia.
Jones, Derek (1987) *Microphones and Muddy Boots*, David and Charles, Newton Abbott.
Mittman, Greg (1999) *Reel Nature*, Harvard University Press, Cambridge, Massachusetts.
Parsons, Christopher (1982) *True to Nature*, Patrick Stephens Ltd, Cambridge.

Wild Film History

Many of the photographs in this book have been found or supplied by Wild Film History, an ambitious new project by the Bristol-based conservation charity Wildscreen to create an online multi-media venue dedicated to the people and productions that have made a pioneering contribution to the development of the wildlife film industry. Visitors to the project's website – www.wildfilmhistory.org – will be able to gain free access to a wide range of landmark films, images and information, as well as a unique collection of interviews with key industry players. Our thanks to Wildscreen and especially to Wild Film History researcher Lucie Muir for her diligence and enthusiasm in uncovering many images that were previously unknown or believed lost.

Index

Entries in *italics* refer to photographs.